Pearls and Knots

D1595422

Pearls and Knots is the story of a generation battling major upheavals. Among the pearls of wisdom and the knotty problems of an era, the reader sees a glimpse of the personal issues entwined in the fabric of life. What is portrayed is the indomitability of the human spirit. What is felt is the beauty of the human condition in a string of universal challenges. Sit and sip a story of resilience—an invigorating tonic for our times!

Kathy DeNicolo — *Connected: An American Homecoming*

I had to remind myself that *Pearls and Knots* is not the ordinary memoir trying to stuff as many past and current issues into the narrative, but a memoir of someone who has lived an American life in the true American spirit. Sarah Schwarcz's story begins with a near-country growing up: playing in the abundance of fall leaves, shedding restrictive girdles, waitressing during college years, then moving on to losing one brother to lung cancer and her second brother—a dedicated, decorated army officer—to the effects of ALS. Sarah is fighting for many years on the side of her beloved husband dealing with multiple sclerosis and other simultaneous debilitating illnesses, after having survived the horrors of years of running and a concentration camp in his childhood.

How much more pain could one person live through and keep their spirit intact? Her memoir is presented in an unconventional but most enjoyable way, with poetry interspersed to lighten the load or enforce one of the heavier points. This book is a good reminder of what the recent past had in store for us, and what might come at us in the near future, while showing us how to cope and still have an enjoyable life.

Peter Slonek — *Who Stole My Father? A Memoir*

Sarah's swift story sprints through two lives bound in breathtaking love. Her spunky youth and school teacher and principal careers primed her to meet challenges with gripping rebounds. The thin-ice path her husband crossed from health to decline from multiple sclerosis is told with both restraint and loving humor.

Judith Marinelli Godfrey — Judith is writing a biography of her father, Radiological Physicist Leonidas D. Marinelli, a leader in the development of nuclear medicine. She is the curator of his collected publications, files, and personal library.

Sarah Schwarcz's *Pearls and Knots* delivers a gripping and lyrical memoir that will captivate readers young and old. Through imaginative storytelling and bejeweled epigraphs announcing each chapter, Schwarcz guides us through the pearls and knots of her life-defining choices and events. We accompany her in a journey from girlhood in Dubuque through her evolution as a poetess and optimistic narrator. Schwarcz's tale is studded with insights arrived through decades of loss and triumph that indulge the senses and satisfy the intellect. As I was guided into realms that rang with the resilience of the human condition, I realized that through Schwarcz, finally I have met a heroine who celebrates the heroic journey from a *wise woman perspective*. A gift for us all in these challenging times. Watch out, Odysseus!

Judy Panko-Reis — *Under the Volcano* (in Shambhala Sun Magazine); *Tango* (in *A Reason to Be Here*); *Chicago's Lost Heaven* (Lewis University Lifetime Learning Review); articles on healthcare disparities for women with disabilities—in 2019 medical journals

This string of wonderful memories from our traveler's childhood in Iowa to grown-up life in Chicago, is lit with Sarah's lyrical prose and poetry—a buoy of love, humor, fortitude, and talent.

Brenda Rossini — *Sherlockian Ruminations from a Stormy Petrel; Graceland Cemetery in Chicago: Unwelcome Passenger on the Ark; A Sherlockian Walk Midst the Tombstones; Mycroft Holmes: Britannia's Master Spy,* (in *Canon Law: Lawyers, Law and the Sherlockian Canon*)

The lilt of Sarah Schwarcz's prose masks her creative magic in transforming Dubuque, Iowa into a fairy tale kingdom. She has written a memoir that is at once personal and universal. Whether writing about delightful challenges or painful trauma, she draws the reader to visualize comparable experiences in his or her own life. Yet this is not a typical memoir. It lacks the staccato presentation of an endless succession of events. Instead, a carefully selected few are allowed to protrude above the author's low-lying clouds of personal privacy. I felt rewarded after reading it.

Richard Davidson — *DECISION TIME! Better Decisions for a Better Life; The Lord's Prayer Mystery Series; The Imp Mystery Series*

PEARLS
and
KNOTS

Dancing on a String
from the Mississippi to Lake Michigan

A MEMOIR

SARAH RAY
SCHWARCZ

PEARLS and KNOTS: Dancing on a String from the Mississippi to Lake Michigan by Sarah Ray Schwarcz

Copyright © 2020 by Sarah Ray Schwarcz

Published by
Hyphen8 Publishing Co.
Libertyville, Illinois, 60048

ISBN: 978-1-7341968-0-1
eISBN: 978-1-7341968-1-8

Cover artist: Samantha R. Haubrich
Cover and interior design by GKS Creative

Faithful threads link to solid sphere memories that linger...
— Mother's Pearls

In memory of their caring natures and uncommon sense,
while treating each day as an opportunity to love and laugh,
this memoir is dedicated to…

Eleanor Huntoon Ray, my sister-in-law, who loved literature
and taught children to love it with all their hearts

Aunt Lillie Branson Washington, who gave me my first two
books—one fiction, one non-fiction—and the desire to teach

Ruth Rotman Silverberg and Sarah Chamberlain Knapp,
who made our lifelong friendship a high art

And to my…
Fabulous first-class children Leigha, Michael, and Michelle,
who can finally take a break from asking me,
"Aren't you finished yet, Mom?"

CONTENTS

Introduction

A Fish Out of Water

W atch it! Keep your line tight. There! You've got it. Hold on. I'll get the net. Don't lose 'er," my life's Muse shouted, as our boat rocked along on the Mississippi River.

He lunged for the crumpled net waiting by the tackle-box, and held it straight out, just as I reeled the line in quickly, swinging the fish up and over the side of the boat. Mine was a deft maneuver for someone who had never fished before. Yet his net's too-narrow aim missed the shimmering walleye. It landed on the deck, flipping and flopping in its death duel with time.

Fishing? Of course not.

Just dancing with a metaphor of my later-life efforts to capture the images, memories and meanings of long-gone moments. I remember the feelings easily. Yet the details slip through the wide-open mesh weave of my writer's net. They taunt me with truth and understanding, staunchly measured against my frequent fog and my questions. Those details escape just a few inches from reach, as they slither over my boat's rail, diving deep into the wide, wide river.

I can hear laughter and a sometime guffaw while they mark their "Ha-Ha, I Win!" high-point scores on my boat's outer hull. Then they swim like crazy downstream to writers from Missouri, who are far more practiced in capture and release. They seek authors whose syntax and grammar and lyricism easily synchronize in grand symphonies to tell tales that cleverly strum words of gold, which only reflect in a few muted sunsets glancing off my shoulder.

"A useless exercise…" one might say.

But that is not the one I will hear. I choose to listen to the melody of a childlike believer, who knows not the difference between fiction and non, and willingly plays in the sandbox until well after dark, long after the supper bell rings.

Dubuque Moments

You know how your hometown always seemed fair-to-middling? Just not the place you would have chosen had anyone bothered to ask you where you'd prefer to grow up. At a certain stage in your life, usually the teen years, it's the place you can't wait to escape. The familiarity, the authority and the rules seem to smother you.

Then one day you reach that magical age of awareness. You look back through today's glasses. You realize your hometown, with its friends and lessons, was your very own *Goldilocks and the Three Bears* right size, on that awesome hill above the perfect river, with the bearable temperatures—most days. If you ever lived in Dubuque, you know many of those days were frigid or mercilessly muggy.

3

Perhaps for some of us, understanding and acceptance never arrive. For me, I think that awareness lived in my head from the moment I left town to attend college. Thereafter, life's busy-ness happened and I returned only for short visits. Absence definitely made my heart grow fonder very early on.

Dubuque roads and sidewalks formed concrete ups and downs—straight ups and very sharp downs. Sliding on clumsy boots down those hills, from home to town, to shop in winter when I was younger, followed by my steady toe on the brakes—except for that one time—on those January hills, once I learned to drive.

I remember trying to taste each individual snowflake as it feathered upon my nose, melting quickly to a brief dart of cold delight on my tongue. High snow slushing over my rubber galoshes which I had been forced to wear that morning, by a protective mother who always won the arguments. There were strong rules-and-views parents back then, trying to squish children into seen, not heard, roles. Some of us resisted, but we learned to pick our battles.

Those were the days of fathers. Fathers had not become 'dads' yet. They did not seek to be friends with their kids. My father left the house for work by six each morning, six days a week, and returned after ten o'clock most evenings. That didn't leave much time for bonding. Maintaining a structural hierarchy in the family was the result of the 1940s and 1950s disciplinary tactics to raise 'good' children. Spoiling was to be avoided at all costs. Yet I don't remember a single time when my father disciplined me. He didn't have to. I carefully avoided crossing any line which would require his participation. Dad was much more involved with the discipline of my two older brothers. I never 'saw' that discipline—but I know it was there. Individual family member privacy was respected in all interactions within the family. High expectations of appropriate behavior caused a high percentage of compliance.

Memory Bytes

Tiny flashes of memories and a precious few keepsakes are all that remain of those early Dubuque years—my green no-speed bicycle, the four-drawer pine dresser given to me by my brothers, my child-size table, Mom's pearls and a few worn jewelry pieces that won't be parted with. Watching my older brother Chuck build his house, helping brush-stain its cedar boards. Fishing the Mississippi while watching the barges drift along with their goods, seeming to move at a luxurious turtle pace, in extreme contrast to cars whizzing by overhead on the Julien Dubuque Bridge to East Dubuque, Illinois. The eight-car pileup on that same dead-fishfly-littered bridge the summer I was nineteen, their slippery winged carcasses forming a treacherous surface as dangerous as our Dubuque snow.

Driving in winters, through that slick frostbite snow over shiny ice-covered roads, with bulky metal chains on our tires, up and down the steep Dubuque inclines. Dumping bushels of our fallen apples over the fence across the street on Fremont, for the farmer's smelly wet-wooled sheep, which had not yet been displaced by urban progress. Long, lazy Canasta-hand summers after all our chores were finished.

Sneaking in a quick Thanksgiving Day driving lesson with my patient brother, Chuck. We were on an errand to pick up Mom's forgotten fruit salad—a salad that promptly flew off the front seat as I hit the curb, having turned the steering wheel too timidly. We salvaged the gloppy pieces that hadn't touched the floor very long and arranged them back in the bowl with great care, laughing all the while.

Each fall, I raked leaf-house designs in our large fruit tree yard, creating outlines of rooms to play in. Toasty smells of burning leaves. Those leaves went up in smoke in minutes, but stayed in my mind for a lifetime. Some memory shots I see as clearly now as back in that 1950s day. I still envision my dad's twelve-to-sixteen-hour workdays at the Coca-Cola plant, sending glass-bottle-packed trucks out on the Iowa, Illinois, and Wisconsin roads, then shepherding them back through the White Street plant garage doors well after dark.

Dad shoveled coal into our home furnace. He and my two brothers, Chuck and Jim, changed storm windows each spring and fall, back when men and women's chores were sharply defined and separate. Only brave 'advance runners' crossed that line, raising eyebrows along the way.

Mom lived in the kitchen or in the basement most days, running endless loads of laundry through the hand-turned wringer, prior to hanging them on outdoor clothes lines. Dryer sheets were not needed. Nothing smelled as sweet as fresh air attached to our clothes. I remember Mom preparing fruit salad with gooey globs of mayonnaise, tipping healthy fare over the border of decent diet sense. Isn't it amazing that back then mayonnaise seemed to be a food staple, akin to milk and bread, in our house with its limited steak meals. No aroma surpassed the delicate smell of my mom's homemade caramel pecan rolls, and pungent sniffs of overdone, peppered meats. Meat that was gourmet rare in those days meant that a mom didn't cook it long enough. It always went back to the kitchen for an added sear to change its color from danger-red to a safe coal-gray.

An outstanding southern baker, Mom could never train me in her magic. A 'pinch of this' and 'add enough flour to make a stiff dough' were too imprecise for me. The one recipe I insisted she give me in writing was for her banana bread—a card I treasure, edges worn and stained with batter dribbles over these many years. As I glance at it today, I smile. True to my memory—it includes all the ingredients except the flour.

We relaxed on prickly plush dust-catcher furniture that matched our heavy chenille robes and fuzzy slippers, which in turn matched the gently worn, soft yellow or pink-striped chenille bedspreads.

Some of the stories were harder to write, took longer to simmer, and involved greater longing for loved ones no longer with me. I was overwhelmed by how to pair my sketchy memories with fact, since fact is often only a ragged, yellow-edged recall, with impressions fading more each day.

When these memories come together, they approach fiction. Yet fiction writers have control of the timing and the results, and the characters and their motivations. The memoirist must rely on the 'feels' of the moments and events, as much as on the truths. Most of us didn't take notes. Shucks!

I was told a brother tossed into the Mississippi River learned quickly to swim. As a girl of the time, my lessons were subtle, disguised as truths unwavering. Only quiet questions were permitted in those days. Prim and proper, seen and not heard topped a girl's behavior chart. That imaginary chart floated in my mind, never written down or posted, yet waving ever strong.

We go through our lives and are bombarded with questions framed as choices, which lead to decisions. Just like those dreaded school tests, we must strategically eliminate the known negatives, select the two most likely, and then often just throw our mind's dice, committing blindly to one of the options, praying there will be no penalty for guessing.

I wish I could say I have always had the ability to choose the correct answer and the perfect life pathway. I also wish that I had perfect memory, and that every single charming thing said, done or experienced by my children, grandchildren, great-grandchildren, relatives, and friends could be gathered in a glass jar just like the fireflies we used to catch on a warm summer night. I am glad I always let those fireflies go, to fly into the night, free from capture.

Just so with these memories. Fly, be free. Light the shadowed night with your love and brilliance. There is no jar large enough.

Mother's Pearls

Markers on a string
Count special moments in a life.
Twenty sets of five
Neatly separated by knots
Which bind them tight.
If one should be lost,
Not remembered clearly,
The knot, jeweler-looped so fine,
Will hold the rest
Firmly on my line.

String, soft and warm,
Shelters the pearls, lustrous and crisp.
Faithful threads link to solid sphere memories that linger.
Which is the jewel,
The pearl or the memory?

The Red Brick House

Stately and square with weathered red bricks, our last-century house sat on a large square lot, with a sturdy square barn off to the rear. I don't even know if the barn stabled animals once, but in my memory it lacks any stalls, so maybe just equipment and tools lived there—some useful, some cast off. The house quickly became part of my seven-to-twelve-year-old self. It thrilled my days. It haunted my imaginative nights.

The backdrop of my world for five wondrous years, the house framed my younger life and even now sends me memory cobwebs which surface each fall, more than any other season. In September and October of my childhood, to my delight and my father and brothers' chagrin, our many trees lost their hold on millions of red, gold, and yellow leaves. In those days, when leaf pickers had two legs, it was a three-week chore to gather and burn the rainbow colors, fading them to charcoal dust.

In the leaf-gathering stage, I was permitted two or three days of architectural design fun, raking the leaves into long snake-pipe piles, to form the outlines of 'rooms' on the surface of the yard, with slanted door-opening lines, much like a blueprint. This activity provided hours of delightful play for me and my friends during those few days. We would drag out our two small children's chairs and table from indoors, to set up a virtual life in the kitchen and parlor of our leaf mansion. We harvested berries, leaves and twigs from the surrounding plants, along with still-moving wooly caterpillars. We threw everything into the pot and pretended to cook our vegetable soup—an earthy organic meal. Based on what I remember we put into it, including stones and dirt, it's a good thing we only pretended to drink.

After the leaves were gathered into their final piles, a delicious golden burnt-toast aroma rose up as the fire consumed them. Each fall since leaving Dubuque, I drive out of my current city, to find that organic charred scent, and when I get it just right, I see my square brick house. I see the leaf-house rows. I see our child's play parlor and pretend kitchen. I hear my mother calling me in before the bats start swooping off the high chimney, narrowly missing my head. Thank heaven my memory stops just short of spoon-tasting that dusty earthen caterpillar-protein soup!

No caterpillars were harmed in the making of this soup.

When we first moved there, my nights were spent devising elaborate reasons why I needed to stay up later, to go to bed when my parents did. Excuse number one: *I've been really good today and deserve to stay up late.* Nope, that didn't work. Number two: *I am coughing and sneezing—cough, cough, sneeze, sneeze— and surely, I need to be checked out?* Still NO. Number three: *I'm not really tired, not tired at all, don't you see?*

Why, you ask, did I not simply explain how frightened I was of the dark, and of those unidentifiable creepy, creaking noises in the old attic, and of those ominous steps thumping ever closer on the wood stairs? Well, if you must know, my childhood was smack dab (that means 'in the middle of' for you youngsters) in the days of stiff upper lip! Family rules and regulations were serious and stood fast, and a rule stated was a rule never broken—you'd break long before the rule did.

Tell my parents I was scared? Ask them to bend a rule? Just the thought of doing that raised the hairs on my neck even higher than did my fear of the night sounds.

The dreaded possibility of contact with the many strange creatures running afoot in my mind fed my nerves nightly. My brain clearly saw a variety of monsters, oozing thick gelatinous drool, following their swallowing of whatever or whoever they just ate, while they chomped at the bit to devour me whole.

The lines between fantasy and reality are not clearly marked in our younger days. Monsters live and breathe our air, and threaten to squeeze the life out of us if we are not ever vigilant.

How many times did you check under the bed when you were a kid? Why does every little kid's bedroom closet door provide exactly the perfect size cover for his very own avocado-green and hairy mind-monster named Fearsome Fred, who is at least twelve feet tall in his stocking feet?

So, those nights, not nearly as much fun as the days, created my escape strategy into books and tales and imagination rationale to quiet my nerves and get me to sleep. Perhaps it was beneficial that I never really came up with that one perfect, masterful, undeniable excuse.

Oh Come, Winged Spring

On the first warm day of spring, you smell dirt and tree buds and fresh grass, and that, of course, jump-starts your thoughts of new beginnings measured against your backdrop of old memories.

My friend Bev and her mom had been kind enough to share a special recipe in my early teen years. Chocolate-covered Candy Nougat Eggs. The candy stores of the fifties had started making them around this time. I had watched Bev's mom make them one day, and I'd spent the following week begging my mother for the necessary ingredients. The urge to create a fantastic dessert had taken hold. Up until now, around age fourteen, I had considered myself an accomplished reader of recipes, a practiced baker of cakes, with pies left to Mom, and meats an unsolved mystery. Due to my years of making fudge and pulling taffy, I was confidant I could duplicate the fancy candy I had seen crafted at my friend's house.

On a warm early spring day, all was ready and the ingredients were spread out on the small pantry counters in orderly array, way before any television cooking show demonstrated the correct way to do it; long before those tiny glass prep dishes placed all your ingredients so artistically on the counter. It was spring, and the storm windows were still on, but you could unlatch the lock, push firmly outward on the storm window, and its metal supports would cringe awkwardly open, just enough to allow a cooling spring breeze to enter the kitchen. The kitchen was heating up quickly, with the creamy candy nougat cooking to the perfect soft-ball stage. On the back burner the chocolate was slowly melting in the double boiler, improvised with one glass pot resting in another, a store-bought unit being out of the question.

When the glistening white nougat and the dark chestnut-colored chocolate were at just the right temperatures, I moved the pots to the pantry counter, ready to make the candies. Feeling the work area still too stuffy, I opened the storm window a little wider for ventilation.

This would be a snap. I'd mold the nougat into egg shapes and carefully dip them in the chocolate, let the drips fall off, and place each oval candy-egg shape on waxed paper to dry. Betty Crocker, move over! Mold…dip…drip…plop. Mold…dip…drip…plop. I think it was on the fifteenth or sixteenth candy egg when it happened.

S P L AT!

Something landed with a sudden swoop, right into the chocolate pot in front of me. I banshee-screamed, froze solid in place, and stared at the pot of mostly cooled chocolate, now straddled by a large inky shape slowly sinking into it.

Mom came running, took one look at the pot, backed away in horror, and told me to get the thing out of there! Now of course, the open storm window, only a few inches behind the chocolate pot—definitely the entrance for this creature—should have been its logical exit. Right?

Wrong! Panicked, I grabbed the thing by the corner of one slippery chocolate-ooze batwing, held on tightly, and ran screaming all the way from the pantry through the kitchen, through the enclosed back pantry, and finally, thankfully, threw it out the back door, tossing it as high and as hard as I could.

It was dark outside. I couldn't see if Choco-Bat flew away, or landed injured in the grass. The next morning, I cautiously checked the yard and sidewalk, but failed to find any bat or chocolate residue. I have always assumed he managed to fly away, probably licking his wings with a huge smile on his face, then begging his own mom for chocolate to melt the following spring.

Did I continue to use the remaining chocolate that day? Of course. As careful as we always were with each and every penny, we would not throw the rest of it away. We removed the top parts that the bat had surely touched.

By the way, the candy eggs were delicious, and became a family tradition for many years. I remember they were wrapped in waxed paper, then packaged in boxes to post to my brother, Jim, in the army.

Remember Porches?

Not inside, yet not quite outside, porches serve to be 'almost' spaces that create comfy atmospheres to enhance our lives. And, just like porches, when you are in these memories of the past, you are not inside them, and yet you are not outside them, either.

My first porch memory is of the faded gray floorboard slats and screens or storm inserts, depending on the season. Next, I almost can feel the old green rocker with the brass nail heads attaching a worn butt-curved canvas seat to a chipped wooden frame. What a soothing safe play area this was. On yard-restricted rainy days, the slightly mildewed air was familiar and calming to pigtailed playmates, with the rain pattering down around us, not on us.

Toy soldiers were in battle-ready positions and placed on and around our mismatched chairs and that one child-height pine table. Older brothers had moved on to high school and then to real war games, leaving these imaginary battles to my friends and me, even though we were girls. On a 1940s air-raid practice night, our porch was off limits, as were lights, conversation, and radios. No television yet.

One neighbor's porch had a swing, perfect for tired little girls who wouldn't give up and go to sleep on summer nights. We'd sit, legs curled under, voices soft, stealing a few more minutes before half-hearted gentle parent bedtime-warnings turned serious, then final.

At the corner house up the hill, one special porch was the entry to each Halloween trick-or-treat night adventure. Dark and cavernous, the black linen-draped vestibule held creepy crawly scary things that seemed alive and threatening. There sat the monster with rubber-gloved fingers filled with ice water, attached to spaghetti-stuffed arms on the make-believe vampire creature of the night. If you survived that porch on Halloween, you were invincible, heroic, super-magic tough.

And we did, and we were, and we all grew up.

Then our family moved, and nothing seemed right at first. This new porch wrapped around part of the front of the house, and extended down the one long mosquito-barrier screened side. Over sixty years old at that time, this comfortably worn porch hosted many Canasta card hands, played out over five summers—long games, with double-deck shuffling. Kids and adults played together, when chores were done. We drank hand-squeezed lemonade and time never seemed an issue.

Another move, to a small duplex with more modern walls at the top of the bluff. Three doors away, a ten-cent ride on the cable car led to that porch, which was a breezeway really, with a boring concrete floor. We ate steaming chili suppers, sitting on modern metal lawn chairs with no ability to body-shape for comfort, in sterile serenity—no romance, no mystery, on this porch of the quickly built, tiny pre-fab duplex of the late fifties.

Just a few doors away, on the eastern Iowa bluff above the Mississippi, my favorite porch looks out over three states—Iowa, Illinois, and Wisconsin. From the height of this sun porch the Mississippi River sews these states together, with the bridges tooth-picking between them, like grown-up professionally-built erector set models.

History and grace seem to reside in this porch, keeping the past alive with reverence for tradition, generation to generation, in my sister-in-law Eleanor's family. On this porch that has existed well over one hundred years, fifth and sixth generation legs scramble over its floor now—my niece Amy's (my brother Chuck's daughter) family. They watch the same-size boats and tugs I saw in the 1940s and 1950s, as I stood looking down that steep bluff toward the Mississippi.

That original porch has competition now, with the family's growth spurring the building of a millennium deck that wraps around its south side, built lovingly and precariously, by Steve and Amy, several years back. The new porch holds more people, yet some days I think it needs weathering, aging like a fine wine, to gain the character of the favorite. More years will help, but it will be hard to match my tranquil feeling while standing on that original enclosed sun porch at sunrise or sundown, fingers warming around a cup of coffee, breaths moving slowly in and out, communing with history and savoring the blessing of time to think.

Off the Rack

I was a tomboy. No one ever called me that, at least not to my face. Back in the 1940s, parents and playmates were not so openly rude. Or, perhaps no one thought of me as a tomboy, because I always wore a dress. But I was a tomboy, both by trade and outdoor nature.

Mom wouldn't hear of letting me wear pants before the age of twelve—right about when the 1940s slid over to the 1950s, and all the other moms had finally given in to seeing their daughters wear sensible pants to play outside. It was a challenge to play baseball in a dress, avoiding those desperate base slides. It was difficult climbing through those half-constructed, sweet-smelling, newly cut timbers erected as the postwar houses rose quickly on the western edge of town, to accommodate the Dubuque sprawl following World War II.

With two older brothers and no sisters, it's no surprise that at the age of six or seven, I chose that sturdy boy-style winter boot. Mom was appalled at my choice. I insisted on those black rubber high-top galoshes with metal latch fasteners —the kind that all the boys wore. A vague memory sits in the corner of my mind—of Mom being mightily embarrassed when my boots got mixed up with those of a classmate—a boy!

When I remember each year's new pair of school shoes—Buster Browns of course, with the size measured under X-ray in that bulky machine—it's no wonder that I wasn't particularly impressed with any shiny, stiff, patent leather little-girl shoes, when dress-up clothes were required. You couldn't bend your feet or run in those dumb things. They were all surface shine, with no soul—pun intended.

I was born about ten years after the onset of the Great Depression, and I grew from age two to seven during World War II, so clothing was more of a reasonably priced necessity than a fashion statement. Fancy accessories and decorations were usually limited to leftover ribbons or lace or buttons. Moms generally sewed and knitted and crocheted.

Families 'made do'. Garbage cans were small, because we threw so little away. You squeezed the use out of every dress hem, letting it out as you grew. You re-soled your shoes. You smiled and said a very polite thank-you when a hand-me-down hit your closet. I lucked out in that department due to only older brothers. Seventh grade sewing class included a wood darning 'egg' for socks—which you practiced on for days at home—learning how to create a perfect weave with thread and needle, to darn your sock when holes magically appeared. Cooking and darning seemed reasonable girl-pursuits back then, but I think the only sock I ever darned was the one that got me an 'A' in that darn Girls Sewing Class!

I have no memory of clothing making any difference in my life other than comfort, prior to seventh grade. Once I reached seventh grade, however, I began to notice color and style and fashion sense—I didn't have any, but at least I was aware it was out there. Our options were limited—no moderately priced items, no Kohl's or Target yet. J.C. Penney and Sears were the choices, with a new concept for those young boys who had a few extra pounds: 'Husky' sizes. No such choices for us girls with a few extra pounds—we just moved up to more adult sizes, and I remember more than one frustrating purchase that made me feel somewhat matronly. Materials were either wool or cotton—no polyester, no spandex.

The worst? Definitely, hands-down, the gym uniform and the girdles! That gym uniform was a railroad boxcar, square of shape and lacking any luster, with zero flexibility. It probably didn't matter anyway, since our girls' gym was a pint-size joke in comparison to the full-size boys' gym, starting in Washington Junior High and on through Dubuque Senior High School. The focus seemed to be heavy on checking that we took complete showers, and very light on appropriate exercise and support for women's athletic prowess. *How our underarms smelled was obviously more important than how those arms threw.*

Now, on to the girdle—a throwback to the cinched-waist corsets of the 1800s that required lacing pulled so tightly that the wearer could barely eat or breathe. Nor, perhaps, express an opinion? The purpose? *I think it was so that females would not break the most important stylish body rule of all—THOU SHALT NOT WIGGLE!*

Forget the discomfort of having one more layer on during warm weather. Forget about the necessity of speed and ease of movement in the restroom. Forget about the funny look of that rubber and metal fixture that held up your nylons—lumping up and showing through any skirt that wasn't a Swiss maiden circle-shape. *Perhaps yodeling was invented to scream out discomfort, rather than a singing method?* Forget about what damage had to have been inflicted on girls' inner organs, being squished into smaller spaces than comfort and common sense should dictate. Trying to squeeze all our Heinz-57 variety bodies into a confined hourglass shape was foolhardy and unhealthy.

Oh, and if I only had a nickel for each leg nylon that I poked a toe-hole or ripped a run into, my 401-K retirement fund would have been secure by the time I was twenty-five!

21

Did any of this shape me? Yes, it taught me patience. It taught me perseverance. It taught me to be one of the first to burn my girdle. It taught me to refuse to follow a crowd when they headed for a cliff. It taught me... to hold my breath for several years until common sense caught up to fashion, and I could safely climb out of that torture rack.

Objects in the Mirror
Are Larger Than ...

I t's a relic. I'm still afraid to use it.

In my eighty years, it has lost only one tiny rose-pink glass chip, and it's older than that, probably by at least fifteen or twenty years. But who's counting—either chips or years?

It sat on Mom's chest of drawers. Large bathrooms with granite countertops didn't exist then. Huge mirrored walls to reflect our faults were not common in homes. No 'selfies' back-dropped in mega-lighting, to catch our new haircuts and share with the world on Facebook. No long Selfie-Sticks to gain just the right angle to showcase our darling dimples. Mirrors to check our faces were more likely to be enclosed in something called a compact, powder puff and all, tucked discreetly into our purses—heaven forbid someone caught you checking yourself out or puffing powder onto your face in public.

Remember when there was a public and a private?

They blend together now, fade in, fade out, no separation lines, like adjacent movie scenes, popping quickly, one on the other. Everyone sees our faults, in typos on social communication channels like Facebook, Twitter, Snapchat and Instagram. In hastily clicked photos to spread upon the world as our messages of worth. Hand on hip, gentle smile just so.

Remember when "Your Mailbox is Full" meant an excited sprint to the porch to grab a handwritten letter to be treasured and reread for several days, months, years.

Just like me, this mirror's pink mother of pearl case shows some wear, with color-engraved edges that are no longer crisp. The single large inset pearl look-alike is slightly chipped, yet still in place. There is a small area of something that does not wash off. I have always left it there. Perhaps it's a bit of nail polish.

When not in use back in the day, Mom's mirror sat face down, perhaps to limit reflecting everything in sight, while people went on with living and reflected long and hard before sending every message and photo into the universe, for all to see.

Enter Otto, Stage Right

WHEN OTTO ENTERED ANY ROOM, everyone knew he was someone they wanted to meet. He was comfortable wherever he was. He made others feel comfortable. Regardless of the occasion or the level of fame of his companions, the camera always delighted in finding him, and he delighted in being the center of attention. Never shy, he said what he thought, and also said what he thought *you* should think. Having experienced so many life-and-death situations during the Holocaust years, he considered anything less than those horrors to be a moment to be treasured, an opportunity to make a difference, a laugh to be shared, or an enjoyment of a lesson learned.

Celestial Moment

Oh, Danny Boy, pray tell,
What is the color of nut brown?
As I see it in my eye, does it match the mud below
Or that deep dark cloud in the sky above
A moment or two before it lets go

Does it mirror the smooth almond
Or the wrinkled walnut
Or the cashew as it curves

Perhaps it two-tones its leathery shape
Hat-topped like an acorn
Born of the Willow Oak

No matter, my true love's hair
Shines forth with crimson glow
As it mirrors my heart
Beating out of its orb
In this celestial moment

When Otto Met Sally

Love is the topic of most stories, movies, conversations and text messages. It is really easy to talk about, and we do that in comfort with those we trust, in snatches of memories, throughout our lives. Yet to put it out there for all to see is daunting.

Hop in. I'll take you for a ride along Iowa's roads in the 1960s. Setting—University of Iowa, in what used to be called a supper club in those days, just outside Iowa City. Time—April, 1960.

Lead characters—Otto, Sarah (I was always called Sally, in my early years.)

Seeking extra funds for the end of my junior year in college, I applied to be a waitress at a restaurant just outside Iowa City. Being cheerful, upbeat and broke, I was precisely the girl they saw as a good hire. I figured the weeks right before and including Mother's Day would provide maximum tips.

The first two weeks went by quickly, and it seemed as though this had been a good decision. I knew my way around food from the many years of baking and cooking at home, and I was with some of my friends in a nice atmosphere for work. The tips would come in handy to close out my junior year on campus and build a little fund to tide me over until I found a summer job back home.

Second semester finals were just ahead. I designed a study and work schedule that even allowed for sleep most nights. Yes, it was ideal. Over the course of the previous six months I had briefly dated three okay-but-not-long-term guys, and had just broken off with the final poor catch.

I had control over my life. Then the cameras started rolling and from stage right, entered Otto. The hostess seated him at one of my station tables. He sat alone.

"Would you like to start out with an appetizer, sir?" I asked with my widest smile and most faked-confidence demeanor. I had already placed the beets, coleslaw, and cucumber relish tray on the table, along with the rolls and butter.

He looked up from reading the menu. I wish I could say that when our eyes locked, I was smitten…but hold on—it's my story, and the cameraman has to reload.

I noticed he took a little longer than most to decide what to order. He asked for specific details about almost every item on the extensive menu. The meal proceeded smoothly. He seemed to like everything I brought out. Nothing remarkable and no takebacks.

What had I noticed about him up to this point? His smile said he was sincere. His eyes laughed when he spoke. His manners were reserved, almost formal. He was impeccably dressed in a business suit.

What stood out each time he spoke? The accent. That somewhere-in-Europe accent, but with an odd Australian-English twist. I was doomed. I think it was the conditioning of the movies of the 1950s. Sprinkled among the many Westerns and dramas were the love stories with the leading men with accents.

And now, right here, captive at my table, was a real live hero with an accent!

I don't think I realized it at the time, but when I look back on it now, I believe it felt as if we had known each other all of our lives.

Easy conversation and funny banter rolled out that evening into the space around us. Now, many years later, I can still see a clear picture in my mind of the two of us, the table, its location in the restaurant, and magically, all other people disappear, as if a spotlight shone only on us.

It was no surprise that as his meal ended and I was clearing the table, he looked up and said quietly, "I travel all week, but I'll be back in two weeks, and I'd like to take you out to dinner." In my prior two weeks of waitressing, I had had at least one or two offers each night to *take me out* and I firmly responded each time that I was a very busy student and appreciated the offer, but had no time just now. Not this time. I thought about his offer, weighed all the personal data about his character that I had assessed with my girl-safety radar, and replied that I had one night free that weekend.

After he left, I replayed the evening as I continued working. While I was concerned, I felt satisfied I had made the right decision. I reviewed his formal manner, his polite conversation, and delightful sense of humor. My radar score told me everything seemed just right.

Then I picked up the tip. Fifty cents. *ONLY FIFTY CENTS?* I lifted the napkin to check under it, and searched through the remaining plates and silver on the table, thinking there must be more somewhere. There wasn't. Okay, okay, stop and think, does the size of the tip really make a difference here? Fifty cents equaled the average amount received for one hour of babysitting at that time, so it's not that it was so awful. It's just that I usually earned more than that for my prompt and efficient service. Was I going to go out with him based on the size of the tip or based on what I felt to be his character traits? I looked directly into my playback camera and voted for the character traits, feeling that tip was a sign of careful spending.

The likelihood of our meeting, falling in love, and creating a marriage and family that lasted forty-three years until death did us part, is somewhat bizarre.

That fifty-cent tip became a well-told joke from then on. I have played the reruns of this evening meal in my head many times over the years, and I always smile in applause.

His Personal Song

Otto loved country music, opera, a little jazz, and didn't mind the Beatles. What he liked most about country was that he could understand the words clearly. Since English was his fifth or sixth language, that understanding was important. How does this explain his love of opera? Opera and country seem to be total opposites. Even his many languages didn't permit him to translate the text of the operas quickly enough for his American-born wife. He had seen those operas often enough that he knew the stories they told, and telling a story is what country music does. Aha … that's their common thread! He developed an early love of the stage and even acted a little himself. Apparently as a young child he frequently sneaked away to involve himself in a play—definitely not considered an acceptable career goal, so family members were not told, I think. He remembered his father knew and supported his interest covertly.

When we first travelled in Iowa as newlyweds, he would sing as we drove along the highway. Otto's voice was excellent—a clear on-key tenor which I found entertaining and uplifting. It made me smile and admire and love him more. He remembered being told as a child that he would have been trained as a cantor, had WWII not interrupted his life and schooling.

It's hard to remember those early days—hard to realize they no longer exist. It was a quiet and friendly time of getting to know each other. Though our backgrounds were extremely different—two cultures, two religions, two parts of the globe—we managed to blend our differences, and even, most times, to cherish them. I think for a long time, though, we each tried to change the other, to make the other into an image like our own, but in the end, we retained our uniqueness. What joined us was our passion to 'do good in our lives', to make a difference. What separated us was the amount of time it took to accomplish that goal in our chosen professions. Otto's fundraising positions required a large amount of evening and weekend work, when lay leaders could meet. My teaching duties, as all teachers know, took up most evening and weekend hours as well.

His love of completely different music genres paralleled his personality. He was soft and dear, yet he could seem harsh and rude at times. He adored people; he aggravated some. He loved his children deeply, yet he had no clue how to provide a steady parenting model, until his illnesses the last eighteen years of his life slowed him down physically, and time came under his control. Leigha, Michael and Michelle were so happy to have him instantly available during this time. As difficult as this period in his life was, it was delightful to see him field their phone calls for advice, now that he was accessible twenty-four hours a day.

Having gone from child to adult so quickly around the age of ten during the desperation of the Holocaust years, he had received no support or understanding of the teenage years. He had no luxury of becoming an adult slowly. He didn't understand why his children weren't mature adults immediately upon their arrival at the age of ten. He was. He loved them, but he hadn't had much time away from work to deal with their everyday needs.

His positions in Jewish Federation of Metropolitan Chicago, Israel Bonds, American Cancer Society and the City of Hope took him from home long hours in the evenings as well as the days. He was passionately dedicated to helping others through his many fundraising jobs. He thrived on setting up the events and dinners that would gain philanthropic support for our communities here and abroad. Giving back was Otto's supreme goal.

Otto's dinner events always brought businessmen, educators, and politicians—on both sides of the aisle—to work together on shared agendas to create funds for research and development of medical and community advances. I will never forget his December 19, 1965, dinner at the Muehlebach Hotel in Kansas City, honoring former Vice President Hubert Humphrey with the Harry S. Truman Commendation Award. Pianist Van Cliburn gave an outstanding piano performance. President Truman gave an earnest speech praising Mr. Humphrey.

Imagine how emotional Otto felt to be 'working with' President Truman, the leader Otto credited with the difficult decisions leading to ending W.W. II, and saving his life! I felt so proud and yet so jittery as I passed through the very serious Secret Service security checks with the other hundreds of attendees. I remember wearing a sale-rack dressy black beaded top over a long black skirt, and thinking throughout the evening how fitting it was that Otto was part of that special moment; but I also remember thinking how much I wished he had not been part of the war years.

Otto was human. He liked clearly drawn opposites. He loved conflict that needed to be conquered. He liked music that told a story of pain and anguish, sometimes resolved, sometimes not. He sang, he cried, he battled the lasting psychological effects of the Holocaust and his final eighteen years of deteriorating health. He never wavered in his search for happiness. I loved him. He loved me. We loved our children and grandchildren. I am so thankful he survived to see all of his grandchildren born. Even when he could no longer walk and was confined to his electric lift-chair, electric scooter and electric bed, he provided the safe 'home base' in our grandchildren's lives.

In those early months after Otto passed away in March, 2003, we would try to keep his memory alive in my two youngest grandchildren's minds. We'd ask Maya, about eighteen months old, what did Grandpa say? Each time she'd make a wonderful 'raspberry' sound with her lips, just like Grandpa did. I'd ask grandson Max, who was four at the time, what he loved best about Grandpa, and he replied with a smile, "He always saved me from you, Grandma!" Max would run up the hallway toward Grandpa's room, escaping my grasp after he'd done some silly deed.

Max knew he was safe in his Grandpa Otto's arms. We all were.

He Never Took It for Granted

I didn't appreciate it enough in 1972. In fact, I remember being rather embarrassed by it. The front yards on our Skokie block usually presented a line of no less than four or five small evergreen bushes, arranged in the usual perfectly symmetrical patterns.

Our house and front yard space were much too small to allow anything additional to the landscape. Otto wasn't house-repair-handy. He liked mowing the lawn and raking the leaves. He wasn't deterred by quick electrical fixes with black plastic wrapping tape. I thought it was rather odd the day that he dug a deep hole in the front yard and mixed concrete to fill it.

Where did Otto find a pole that size? I never asked him. I only think of that question today. He set the pole in the ripening ready-set concrete, and stood there for a time, holding the pole upright until it held. Amazingly, when he let go, the pole stood straight, really straight. It dwarfed the house and seemed out of place there. He flew his prized American flag every clear day for the next couple of years, in front of that tiny Skokie bungalow, with the thirty-foot wide front lawn.

Forty years ago, we'd leave that home, around the Fourth of July, and head for Glenview and more space for our growing kids. I was born in this country. He wasn't. I frequently took our flag for granted. He never did. Yes, it was a part of my life, yet it was usually hanging limp on a stage corner at my school assemblies and commencements, not windblown and waving freely. But in Otto's mind for those next few years, and bigger than life on our front lawn, that flag flew high, bravely rippling, even on still days, sending out you-can-do-it signals to guide our way.

He spoke six languages. His American flag spoke only one. Freedom.

The Sights that We Saw Near Washington Street

THE FOLLOWING STORIES AND POEMS were written in or near Gurnee, Illinois, from 1996 – 2005. Thank heaven for the thoughtful neighbors (particularly Greg and Meg) in this young community—who spent time with Otto and me. It kept Otto going for seven more years. Gurnee is where Otto and I built a home to accommodate his mobility needs— wheelchair-height counters and tables, accessible deck and oversize bathroom with roll-in shower—all those things that supported his daily life as a courageous survivor in the face of the physical and mental challenges of multiple sclerosis, diabetes, and heart and lung impairment. Everything in our lives revolved around his medical issues. We really couldn't afford this house. Yet, accessibility needs dictated that we certainly couldn't afford *not* to build it. I had already downsized with great thought twice in the previous ten years—making two budget-conscious moves that met some of his needs. Each time, a downturn in mobility necessitated an upturn in location, and required rethinking. The final catalyst was when Otto became lodged upside down one morning on the floor of our tiny bathroom's shower, requiring the paramedics to cut out the vanity cabinet, to access him, following his slip off his shower chair. Do it right the first time...a lesson repeated, unfortunately, over and over in my life. I think I've got it now.

Our ability to travel anywhere, even for a short period, was curtailed. Our new home provided Otto with an oasis for travelers to visit us, as his roads narrowed. For those first five years, he was able to maintain a fair amount of independence in comfort and safety, while I was still able to work in nearby Chicago and Mundelein. In his last two years, as the multiple sclerosis and diabetes and circulatory issues gained ground and he could no longer make safe transfers on his own strength, we needed full daytime help.

Sometimes it was difficult to capture any small moments to cherish in the face of the many health setbacks. But we learned to face them together, and when each curve ball hit, we devised some type of antidote to avert it. Our shared antidote for the hard times was writing. Otto wrote some of his history. Thank heaven for computers at this time in his life. They allowed him to interact with the world at large. Early in the 1990s, he learned to two-finger type, and he communicated in the earlier Internet medical forums with others who had multiple sclerosis.

His communication with those who shared his medical problems was both a help and a hindrance. Doctors' solutions and the home treatment remedies available at that time were severely lacking in any tested or proven success. MS patients and their doctors were grabbing at anything that might force those legs to stand again. We even tried a lengthy regimen of chemotherapy sessions to diminish the autoimmune reactions of his system. On his final trial session, he would endure three severely debilitating weeks out of each month, over those two years. We also tried several massive medication therapies and multiple physical therapies, none of which helped. They were expensive and weren't covered by any insurance. Most created new problems of their own. The more responsible websites were not yet posting any reliable medical information.

After a while, we decided the Internet's information wasn't therapeutic and it frequently disturbed Otto, so he eventually drew back on his own. Whew! This was not nearly so hard as the day he knew he wasn't able to drive anymore. That realization came on the day of another serious fall, which landed him wedged between the car and the concrete block wall in our very narrow condo garage. No longer being able to drive came close to breaking his spirit for a while, yet even that he survived. He accepted one more independence signpost falling to the wayside, as his multiple sclerosis disease forged ahead, rapidly destroying the myelin membrane protecting his brain and spinal cord nerve pathways, consuming their portability and limiting movement throughout his body.

Washington Street cuts an east-west path through the center of Gurnee and has the job of moving a heavy traffic flow from Round Lake through Grayslake through Gurnee, ending in Waukegan at the western edge of Lake Michigan. It is farm field, suburban houses, and Six Flags Great America pathway. Since this route connecting our daughter Michelle's house and mine was well worn—with me helping with her children, and Michelle and her husband, Steve, helping with Otto—Washington Street became the focal point of several of my 'observation' writings. I wrote the Fog poem to capture Otto's and my struggle to keep going through adversity, even on the many days we couldn't see clearly ahead of us.

Fog, Pounce-Ready

With Thanks to Sandburg and Frost

The fog comes on little cat feet
"Hello?!?! I don't think so."
Not in my Metropolitania, it doesn't.
Fog comes on leopardous, treacherous paws.

Haunches wired tight, pounce-ready and thunky.
In keeping with the modern age
It seems like it has built-in radar
Made for asphalt-jungle routes.
Or is it just focus-beamed to my gray car?

If I didn't have places to go and promises to keep,
I'd let it win today's match.
I'd watch it snarl and snare the Chevys and trailer semis,
"And leave my Ford alone, thank you, sir!"

Maybe in the old days of country roads and forests far,
The cat motif would fit.

THE SIGHTS THAT WE SAW NEAR WASHINGTON STREET

"Not now. No, not now!"
Today's fog devours two cars in front of me,
Then turns, licks its chops, and sneers,
As I narrowly escape its grasp.

If only it would hold stock-still,
I could aim my car for its chest,
Catch it on my grill,
And toss it high, back to that tree,
Saving mankind for my Saturday feat!

But no, just as I thought
I had it caught,
It slithered 'round my bumper,
And lock-jawed the Jeep behind me.

Oh, well, Mankind must fend for itself once more,
For, yes,
"I have promises to keep,
And leaping over leopards wasn't on my list of things to do today."

Tackle First, Think Later

Cold, wet, and heavy, the snow kept coming, slowly paced at first, then gathering speed, until there was no way to avoid it, if you wanted to stay on top of the task. This snowfall was predicted to be a big one. Keeping our handicap van ready for any emergency was a prime priority. Determined not to give in or let the storm get ahead of me, I forged a small path with the only tool at hand, a grandchild's toy shovel—one that should have been put away before this season started.

Stinging crisp flakes on my face, breath freezing almost before exhale, fingers and toes with perhaps twelve minutes left in my sixty-year-old-body batteries, I moved forward furiously— stroke, push, lift, stroke, push, lift, until the car's front bumper surfaced. At the precise moment when I reached the snow-piled rear bumper, I noticed the eerie quiet behind the wind's wail, and paused to look up the street, then down. Twice. Then I checked a third time. Odd, the forty-year-olds weren't outside yet, not one. They waited. They waited until it stopped, until they knew exactly what damage was done and where to start, probably so no wasted effort would be expended.

By contrast, I have always preferred the headlong start, the battle begun, my unknowns charged, before they could win by default. Perhaps the forty-somethings are smarter after all. I know Otto would have been out there with me, if he could have invented a way to affix a snowplow to his electric scooter. I had sneaked out before he woke, or his common sense would have prevented my battle.

Knee High

I pass you each day,
each way.
You wake
in Spring, dark rows
converging to wheel-spoke centers.
Earth moist, chunky, like huge chocolate waffles.
Morning trip—nothing yet.
Expectation, a soft suggestion of
about-to-happen.
Nothing yet.
Evening ride,
perhaps I see one.
Brown earth, sunny day, baked
toasty warm.
Telltale green 'V' shoots,
dainty jolly green giant fingers peeking through.
Timid sprigs today,
in seven days, a full field.
In ten more years,
progress and pavement will win? "Please, no"

Washington Street

Perhaps I need another route,
perhaps this path's too tried and true.
It dips and sways just gently so,
our minds wander way too much, to and fro.

Concrete, cornstalks, roller-coaster partner,
four-lane glue of pavement and pasture.

The street's so straight most of the trip,
that one curve seems dishonest, almost a trick.
They spent some time reshaping nature,
raising the landscape, a safety feature.

But wouldn't you know, man's talents fall short?
Tortoise still thought its path he could cavort.

The truck swooping swiftly,
three cars close behind,
"Can drivers see me waving?
Perhaps there is time!"

"No, No! Don't stop and back up!"
Not Tortoise, nor driver, has options here.
But stop and back up, the truck driver did,
and slowly Tortoise forward did bid.

I slowed to a crawl,
fearing certain disaster.
Will truck meet tortoise,
sending him to the Hereafter?

I check my rear mirror.
Hear that burned rubber screeching?
Traffic comes to a very quick halt,
answers my up-sent prayers beseeching.

And then, just as suddenly as begun,
Mother Nature and Tortoise had once again won!

Yellow Belly, Black Wings

MONDAY
Yellow belly, black wings
Feather-puff light
Swaying gently, facing west
Perched high
Flits away when I go by.

TUESDAY
Yellow belly, black wings
Same branch, sky high.
Faces south, flutters briefly
Swings north
Secret launch, soars forth.

WEDNESDAY
Yellow belly, black wings
Anguished cry, same branch.
Sundial's choice points east now,
Eagle swoop!
Sharp turn, terror loop,
Fly! Fly! Fly!

October Sky,
Thanksgiving Nigh

Almost waited too long
Pretended they'd stay tight
To the trees forever.

Grabbed my grand-munchkins
Brown, auburn and blond
For Grandma's trip to the forest,
Singing off-key as we drove along
"If you go out in the woods today…"

Old feet in gym shoes chase
Young toes in sandals
Playing hide-and-seek behind oaks and maples.
"Do you see it—do you see it there?"
"What do you mean? What? Over where?"

"High, so high, stand tall, look up."
Apple-red, burnt-orange, lemon-yellow buttercup.
Crayon colors for us today,

THE SIGHTS THAT WE SAW NEAR WASHINGTON STREET

Look quick, they'll fade away.
"I see it!" "I see it!" "I see it, too!"
Way up, bright leaves stick against sky blue.

Thankful they see them, almost the same
As those I knew when I played their game.
Thankful they smell it—the warm charred-smoke smell,
As I remember, when I could run and jump as well.
Thankful they touch them, with round eye wonder,
And find them smooth, edges crisp or turned under.

Thankful they stop suddenly
To listen to forest silence.

It's a year-round thing you see, so daily thankful be.
October colors burst free before November chill,
Painting mind scrapbooks to browse, through winters still.
Thanks for brown, auburn, and blond.
Apple-red, burnt-orange, lemon buttercup, sky blue,
Colors crisp, smells sweet and sour,
Hugs cheery and true.

Sugarplum Pink

Froufrou – that's it, froufrou.
Under three feet high, pink tights
Pink tutu, pink slippers, sunburned pink cheeks
Almost four-year-old knees wobbled stage right
Then left, only a half-second off the beat
Butterfly-light to the '40s music.

Holding our breath as she pliéd daintily forth
Slipping solo into every Granny and Grampa's hearts
Hair tightly knotted with crepe-paper posies.

Five in her row now
Feet out, tummies in, hands up, twirl right
Ten slippers turning-counting-counting-turning
Toes pointing sharply
Deep bow.

After she received her
Delicate flower basket reward,

THE SIGHTS THAT WE SAW NEAR WASHINGTON STREET

"Mommy, why did everybody laugh at me?"
"We weren't laughing at you
We couldn't help but smile
Because your serious face
Won us over by a mile!"

Deck the Deck
with Hooves So Jolly
Fa-La-La-La-La

The winter holidays always caused some agonizing questions of appropriateness throughout our marriage of forty-three years. How do we celebrate within a framework of joy, balancing yet not offending, gathering but not dismissing? I'm sure I'm not alone when I say there was always a feeling of being out of the mainstream during the preparation and decorations of Christmas. We lived a Jewish life, joyfully celebrating Jewish Holy Days and traditions. I remember having difficulty that year finding our Menorah to hold the Hanukkah candles. It was definitely a miracle that we came up with a solution— we lined up four pairs of graduated-height separate candlesticks, with one single one in the middle as the Shamash (the candle that lights other candles) and they stood proudly on the ledge above the kitchen counter, viewable in the living room and up the hall in Otto's first-floor bedroom, as well.

As Otto's health deteriorated at a faster pace from 2001 to 2003, I became bolder, yet still cautious. He required greater care in his final two winters. Otto had become housebound and eventually room-bound for the most part, due to the need for one, sometimes two, helpers to safely transfer him from lift-chair to scooter to electric bed.

His room window looked out on our backyard of trees, on the lot that we had selected in 1996, for its natural beauty year-round, compact but beautiful. That choice was so right, though beyond our means. The backyard was a mini-forest, standing mostly shaded, but with sprinkled sunlight always drifting down into the dark spaces, three seasons of the year. It gave Otto a great view, just when his views were severely narrowing. As the dark winter of 2001-2002 approached, I made a trip to the hardware store, seeking some 'religiously neutral' decoration that would light up and be visible to him, through our first floor windows. I previewed and dismissed one-by-one, all the Christmas trees, the strings of lights, the Santa Claus blowups, the reindeer...

AHA, that's it! The deer!

I selected a buck and a doe. I placed them out in our mini-forest, on the red gravel path our son, Michael, had designed and constructed for us after we moved in, so that Otto could experience the backyard, riding his scooter. The buck stood quietly upright, proud and bright, his antlers announcing strength and dominance. The doe moved—well, at least her neck and head moved—back and forth or up and down, I can't remember which. *I certainly know that in our marriage my head moved up and down much more than back and forth, but if Otto were telling this story... he'd probably say the reverse.*

The first night I connected a long extension cord to our 'Hanukkah Deer' and lit them in the backyard, then showed them to Otto, and waited for his reaction. His eyes sparkled, just like the deer's twinkly bulbs, and I knew I'd scored a ten! We shared many laughs about our Hanukkah Deer, and they brightened a very long winter that first year, and then they hibernated in our garage over the summer. Our neighbors probably wondered why the Schwarczes up the block finally put holiday features in their yard. The winter of 2002-2003 saw severe deterioration in Otto's health and mobility, and as December approached and the days shortened, I wondered what to do with the deer. Otto wouldn't be able to see them much because he was spending more and more time in his bedroom, and they were barely visible from his bed or electric lift chair. His bedroom was on the first floor, and our backyard was much lower.

Of course, the deck! That's it. I'll put them up on the east side of the deck, and his bed faces that way, and they will be visible.

They came. He saw. We conquered.

Our Hanukkah deer enjoyed their new residence, I believe. Otto's spirits were buoyed by their twinkling lights, right outside his window, through that winter. I like to think I would have moved them into the house the following winter, if I'd had the chance…

Family Memories

ON FIRST READING, THESE STORIES have a sad undercurrent, ranging from the impact of the long, devastating WWII years, to the health ravages. Some of the stories were harder to write than others. I stalled for a few years, overwhelmed by how to pair my sketchy memories with fact, since fact is often just a ragged, yellow-edged recall of impressions; at least one short block closer to truth, but fading a little more each day.

Family memories come in spurts, triggered by a date or question or thought flashback that permits you to select the puzzle pieces that fit the whole, or perhaps just allow you to savor one all by itself. As you get older, life's immediate intensity has diminished somewhat, and the lessons of value remain in your comforting quilt, sewn together in the relationships formed with those you knew and loved. Sometimes the hardest part is to let go of the moments and words that wounded, allowing you at least to forgive if not forget, hoping your quilt remains soft and supportive, colorful with cherished patches, soothing to the touch of memory.

Please don't walk away with sorrow and despair as the message of worth. Instead, be inspired to seek your own strength of character, endurance, respect, and humor to face your challenges, on any side of an ocean, any year in your life. Our family's brave souls have walked very treacherous roads before you—some exterior, some interior. With perseverance, they stayed the course, and sprinkled sturdy, blessed breadcrumbs for you to follow.

My Wizard, Chuck

In my mind, my brother Chuck, twelve years older than I, always lived in a merit-badge Boy-Scout-beige character suit. He gave me my first nickname, Pinky, based on my pretty pink ruffled bloomers, so I was told. Pinky was soon to be followed by Sally—probably when I outgrew those bloomers.

We didn't share toys. I had two older brothers. Their toys were pretty much off limits. Not just because they were older. Boys played with boy toys. Girls played with girl toys. In my mind, 'competent and successful' mirrored what older boys did. I didn't much care for dolls and frilly things. No one else in the house played with dolls, so I didn't think they were very important. Persons I looked up to were guys. They were the doers—heroes on the movie screen and heroes in real life. Independent girls were only fictional characters in a Nancy Drew mystery in a library checkout bin, at that time.

Probably anything Chuck would have held dear in those days—the early 1940s—would be on the danger-recall list today. Products were not labeled with factory warning stickers. Parents were expected to provide sensible safety rules and oversight. Kids up and down the block on Nevada and Fremont Streets in Dubuque, Iowa, were expected to exercise pre-thought, followed by appropriate play and responsible acceptance of consequences, if something ever went awry. In short, we were expected to think. We devised our own games with neighbor kids throughout all seasons.

If something did go wrong, we tried to fix it ourselves. To ask a parent for help was only a last resort. It meant 'failure'—the "F" word of those times.

I thought of Chuck as a brilliant resource. When he sat still, which wasn't often, I remember books surrounding him. Fiction and technical manuals supplied equal joy. He learned new skills in every decade, including learning to pilot a plane after he hit fifty, soaring over the Tri-State corners of Iowa, Wisconsin and Illinois.

He was never there as much as I wanted. This describes my feeling of perpetual loss of this special brother at crucial times throughout my life. By the time I was five, he had entered the Navy, as so many young men did prior to graduating high school, to save the world from destruction. This was right before WWII ended, thankfully, and he came back to us—safe, but grown up. I was six. He was eighteen. We had nothing in common except respect and love.

After the war, Chuck worked with my dad, the manager at the Coca-Cola Bottling Company, down on White Street, in Dubuque. From his twenties, he operated and maintained the bottling machinery, learning on the job. He could fix, design, or improvise absolutely anything.

I always remember him with a book in one hand, a wrench in another, a fishing pole in another, a boat steering wheel in another, and an airplane half-wheel in another. Oh, and I almost forgot, ski poles in another. And yes, Chuck seemed to have more hands than anyone. He taught himself everything, by reading complex technical manuals or using plain old Chuck-sense.

If he grew bored, he'd investigate and build or solve something. And, of course, in his spare time, he kept the historic funicular railway Fenelon Place Elevator (in his wife Eleanor's family) running smoothly up and down the steep bluff, oiled and ready. Also known as the Fourth Street Elevator, it was first listed in the National Register of Historic Places back in 1978. He reconstructed its overlook deck to safely accommodate all those "active kids from Chicago" on their fieldtrips. Having four wonderful girls of his own—Amy, Cynthia, Barbara, Daphne—he knew the importance of safe environs for children.

My world dimmed when he left us too soon at age sixty, felled by lung cancer. During my whole busy life, I had always visualized our later years—when maybe I could catch up in maturity—and we would both have time to escape life's over-programmed twenty-four-seven, to sit and reminisce on that Dubuque porch.

I had always mused that when we were older and could slow down, Chuck would finally have the time to reveal the secrets of the universe to me. I was certain he knew them all, though his humility would cause him to deny that.

So many unanswered questions...

Too few days to ask.

My Hero, Jim

How do we measure time? In our younger days, time stretches on forever and always seems available. In my memories of those luxurious long days, when I could talk directly with my brother Jim, who was five years older, I always knew he was my hero. Even before he enlisted in the army in 1952, served in the Infantry, trained with the 82nd Airborne Division, served in the Quartermaster Corps, and attended Officers Candidate School at Ft. Benning in 1955. Well before he floated down to earth on multiple jumps, and thankfully, his backup chute opened, after the first one failed in a training session. Before he helped in the cleanup of the Korean War. Before he was stationed in France, trained troops in Ethiopia; before he completed numerous helicopter reconnaissance missions in Vietnam.

I knew he was my hero, from the way he lived his life, and from the respect and love he provided me and his family.

Then we both married and raised our families and time flew with laser speed to the fateful day when amyotrophic lateral sclerosis was finally diagnosed. Jim was a brave soldier who served with dedication and honor, helping to shape the lives of fellow soldiers. Jim survived many tours of duty over the globe, but he had only a few years of relaxed retirement, prior to his honored ceremony in the Fort Myer Chapel at Arlington National Cemetery. In his retirement he worked hard in several endeavors, including real estate, veterans' employment and logistics consulting. He was near-professional level in his lifelong golf game.

Jim returned home from Vietnam a year or two before the worst of the rejection and scorn for our returning soldiers started to play out. Nothing could ever make up for the lack of celebration or appreciation for their service that our Vietnam veterans received, in that horrendous, drawn-out conflagration. They came home filled to the brim with their wounds of body and spirit. I am glad Jim was never confronted directly with the hatred that this war engendered, but it hung over so many of our veterans. Our country's bureaucracies and our citizens' wills and divergent thinking formed a never-ending angry and apathetic stage, strewn not with flower petals and ticker-tapes, but with suspicion and derision, and worst of all—quiet.

Such quiet. It was deafening.

Families still hugged and blessed their returning loved ones, of course, but the horrors of war, the mistakes on the field and some decisions of military and civilian leaders, took their toll. That toll landed heavily on the shoulders and minds of our soldiers. They did their jobs with such determination and expertise. I am always left with the belief that a medal for the life of a fallen soldier seems a very poor bargain.

FAMILY MEMORIES

I have never lost the strong visual and emotional memory of my visit to the Vietnam Memorial in Washington, D.C., with Jim. As we walked the dramatic physical and mental length of that powerful memorial in profound silence, I watched him search the engraved names for soldiers he had known and lost. As he read through the long lists carved into the wall, he found one name of a very close friend. I could only imagine the pain Jim experienced each day as he rebuilt faith and hope upon his return. During Jim's offshore service years, I cherished the letters from his wife, Jane. Her wonderful letters detailed the basics of their lives, centering on the usual family *over here* happenings, while he was experiencing several difficult tours of duty *over there,* some in helicopter missions in the jungles, to save our soldiers.

While Jim's name is not on the Vietnam memorial, he definitely was a victim of that war, as all its soldiers were, even those who returned physically unscathed from the battlefield. Agent Orange, to which he was possibly exposed, has proven to be a causative factor producing deadly effects, among them Lou Gehrig's disease—amyotrophic lateral sclerosis. Jim began to show signs of this disease in his late fifties (the early 1990s) and, true to this disease's most usual course, he was gone in two years, at age sixty.

From his service years in the 82nd Airborne 1953-55, to Officers Candidate School, 1955; to the Korean War tour 1956-1957; to France 1959-1962; Ethiopia troop training 1965-1966; England 1967-1969; and Vietnam 1970, Jim applied a brain that approached all problems with a thorough knowledge of math and science, and a deep respect for logical thinking. I remember how frustrated he felt each time his world and the world at large didn't operate according to that same logical standard of reference.

From the day in 1952 when he enlisted in the Army, he excelled in training and leadership and in choosing a wonderful wife. The many moves with their three sons, Robert, Ronald, and Kevin, across the United States and the world were a lesson in patience and cooperation, with dedication to ingenuity and honorable service. I always laugh when I remember Jane's stories of their cross-country car trips, accompanied by large glass dual-service peanut butter jars, prior to oasis stop days.

Among other awards, Jim received the Bronze Star, Meritorious Service Medal with Oak Leaf Cluster, Army Commendation Medal with Oak Leaf Cluster, Legion of Merit and three awards for his valor in Vietnam.

When Jim's service ended, he engaged in community activity and further education. He belonged to the Veterans of Foreign Wars and American Legion. He was a member of the Fort Belvoir Golf Club and a past treasurer of the West Springfield Village Civic Association, in Virginia. Jim graduated from the University of Maryland in 1962, and earned his master's degree in Management Information Systems there, in the early 1990s.

When not in combat, his life as an officer allowed some time to develop a love and skill for golf, a game he finally had some free time to pursue during the early years in retirement, before the disease consumed his coordination and voice, leaving his brain and his will intact.

I don't remember enough of our childhood interactions. Our interests and friends didn't match. I remember his smile, his smarts, his and Jane's care for my mom in her difficult late-life challenges. I cherished the presents he gave me with his generous heart and hard-earned money, still a child himself. I remember his teasing of me being adopted—a joke he and Mom enjoyed once in a while, probably due to my outspokenness.

I remember his initiation of our family reunions in Virginia in the early 1980s, with buckets of crabs covered in golden butter that slid down our chins while we leaned over outdoor deck rails, savoring the Atlantic at dusk. He enjoyed cooking and eating good food accompanied by good wines. I can still taste the Japanese Sukiyaki he made after his return from Korea in the 1950s.

It is hard to avoid my sad thoughts of his final overwhelming two years, 1991-1993, as he battled A.L.S. There were minimal therapies or medications then, and it remains a difficult disease to this day. On one of my visits, I remember a long ride his brave wife and I took down a country road in Maryland, to purchase a live beehive that was set up outside a window, and vented through the window to the inside. Jane captured individual bees with tweezers, to sting him on his chest, back, legs and arms—on acupuncture points. The purpose of this suggested regimen was to hope the bee venom would activate his immune system's white blood cells to fight the disease. Perhaps this stalled the inevitable progression; at the very least, it gave us all a few more months of hope that he could win this battle. When families exhaust the options that regular medical practices can offer, they seek alternative therapies that might have a measure of success.

On a cold January day in 1994, Jim was laid to rest in Arlington National Cemetery. The words of General Billy J. Stalcup honored Jim in memory of his dedication and military service. The General's eulogy gave exceptional insight into Jim. Those words helped us view Jim in his outstanding career, but mostly they highlighted for us all, the fine soldier we lost with his passing.

When you visit Arlington, history and humanity come together in sharp images. You always feel a quiet reverence, even when the silence is broken by the sharp three-volley rifle shots of the honor squad, fired for newly fallen heroes who gave their best.

The words. The rifle shots. The tears. The smiles through the years.

Never forgotten.

Between the Raindrops

What a difficult time. I took her doctor's advice. I didn't question back in 1975. Was it right? I don't know. It seemed there was no choice at the time. I still had faith that others knew more than I, and I didn't trust my own heart. Looking back, knowing what I do now, I know I would have made a very different choice. I certainly have regretted that path all these years later. Her doctor said it was time to get her more care, based on her serious fall and her inability to care for herself. The importance of independence was a key my brothers had discovered earlier than I. I just wanted her safe, social, and fed nutritious fare. I wanted her quiet and lonely life to change to what it could have been.

So, I raced all over Dubuque, seeking just the right place for Mom, where there would be activities that would awaken her mind, friends who would keep her active and interested. My mother had never gone outside the family for friendship. She used a remote control for the television, and a very remote control for her life. She held neighbors at a distance. I remember her gentle reminders to keep my own counsel, to create what seemed to be protective space bubbles. I will never understand the why of that. I don't know the stories that caused those protective behaviors. Armed with today's knowledge, I would have explored these behaviors with professional medical and psychological resources.

What were the reasons no one except family ever came to our house for gatherings or celebrations? She had been the youngest in a large family. Perhaps there was no need for her to go outside of that family unit. Perhaps the friendlier South contrasted so much with the more reserved northern patterns where I was born, that she never recaptured a warmth of attitude or friendship in the North. Perhaps the lack of family members around her, once she moved North, proved overwhelming.

What illness or events closed off this woman with such a delightful and bright sense of humor within our small family? She neither invited nor was invited. What levels of trust had been betrayed? Within our family, we took our closeness as normal, and we didn't question. Today, I would question. I would resource. I would fight that withdrawal. Back then I didn't dare question. I was a follower. I operated within the perceived parameters set silently, yet with great binding power.

Though my mother was seventy-one on that day of admittance to the nursing home, her face remained a beautiful soft and young surface, smoothed by the years of nightly Ponds or Jergens facial cream rituals. I think southern ladies learned early that sun damage might be held at bay by daily slathers of cream; even inexpensive jars served as worthy gladiators. Her still-curly hair had faded to salt-peppery wisps with time's march, yet remained perky in contrast to her slowed walk and slower thoughts. This woman with such strong beliefs of correctness in all her previous years, now acquiesced with no thought of challenge. Today, this would be a clear warning sign to take alternate action. Back in 1975, it spurred me to solution based on safety, with my personal sentiment ignored bravely, thinking my tears only selfish, and therefore, to be ignored.

I tried the best nursing home location recommended, but the finances wouldn't fit. I located one that was older, but seemed clean and cheerful, and listed loads of outings and activities. In one week, her move to the nursing home was accomplished. She seemed cheerful, and I like to think relieved.

On the day Mom moved in, I stayed for a long time, to talk and help both of us relax with this change, making sure her clothing and personal items were organized neatly in the storage cupboards provided. Then I headed down the hall, through the front screen door, and stood under the porch overhang for a minute.

Rain began to fall, picking up intensity quickly on that warm late-summer day. I decided to wait until the rain let up. I stood there for more than a few moments. I felt someone exit the screen door behind me, and close it quietly. Not looking up, I sensed rather than saw the young man. He, too, waited. The rain started to let up, but I didn't think it was time to go yet. I was still waiting, watching the rain. I felt him move just slightly toward me. Then he paused and spoke.

"Run, just run *between* the raindrops…"

I turned and took a clear look at him. He was a beautiful young man, with Down Syndrome, dressed neatly in summer khakis. He had arrived in my life at that exact time, to deliver a brilliant oration, its profound meaning cocooned into those six encouraging words of hope and survival. I smiled a thanks, then took his advice and ran down the porch steps to the parking lot, crying my larger-than-raindrop tears.

Numbers – Too Many to Count

Bella's tiny, frail, almost feather-like posture comes to mind at first when I remember her. My second thought, however, frames that staunch resilience, measuring at least twice her eighty-seven pounds. Her cane was always there, used for ups and downs into chairs and across pavements over her world travels. More often, it hung stiffly upon her wrist, frequently unused as she walked, and we sometimes made quiet jokes about this each time she left us.

The visits of my husband's mother were never easy. She wanted to visit, wanted to know us, and to be known by us. But the gates and the locks on her mind had become more intricate as the years wore on. The inhumane enemies had come close to dispensing with her physical being, as evidenced by her chest-to-hip brown leather body brace. The brace stood upright each night, on a chair by the bed, sentry to her sound sleep, a rest well-earned after the years of torture and running, many sleeps ago.

After our initial hugs and greetings, we measured our children— Leigha, Michael, and Michelle—next to her, to see how they had grown. Then our conversations began. When we were on everyday topics, we were in safe territory. Words flowed, we smiled and laughed aloud, and all of us treasured our peaceful interchange.

Some days this tranquil harbor of family chatter lasted thirty or forty minutes, but less was usually the case. Her eyes, such a pale blue, bordering on gray, seemed to stare into the distant past, and her mind and our imaginations would follow her tortured trail to central Europe —Czechoslovakia, Hungary, Germany—the road back to the war.

Before and after World War II, my brain found it impossible to imagine such evil forces ever again impacting on so many lives at one time. Numbers lost were not countable. Indeed, by the time of Bella's capture, the tattoo numbering on the arms of Jews was no longer happening—the evil was so large, too large to accurately count those being murdered.

"Those murderers…they couldn't kill all of us…they tried, but some of us, some of us remain. No, it's too awful to speak…the world had to have known, yet nothing…my husband…the numbers…my family…the camp…"

The phrases came quietly, murmured in short spurts, the words not matching the violence of the acts. Her thoughts seemed disjointed. Her psychological pain weighed heavy in the room.

Then, just as suddenly as it began, the road to her past curved back to the present. Her eyes refocused on her surroundings, and the supper preparation and cooking sounds and smells brought her back to the evening. Back to us.

Our children—at some point in these moments—would quietly drift away to play, not understanding exactly *where* she was, thankfully.

My favorite memory is of seeing her pray, at dawn and dusk, her chanted 'davening' barely audible to our ears, just loud enough to reach G-d's ears quickly, her piety sincere.

The cane that hung on her wrist, just in case she needed it, had accompanied her from Pittsburgh, her American home, to Chicago many times over the years. Her survival rations—tea with a little sugar, toast, occasional small portions of chicken soup, small pieces of challah bread—took her to eighty-eight years, many of which were spent in the past, reliving the horror.

Just like her cane, Bella was straight, strong, unbending. The cancer that finally ended her battles was an internal invasion. She always managed to withstand each challenge from the outside.

How Not to Have
a Heart Attack

Picture this. I was the principal of two K-8 Chicago Public Schools—Solomon and Sauganash—one and one-half miles apart. There were several hundred students between them. I spent each workday racing back and forth, tending to needs. Whenever there was a crisis at one school, guess where I was? Of course, at the other. On this day I was at the Sauganash school, on the north side of Chicago.

Time—approximately 11:30 a.m. Year—1988. Telephone rings. Otto calling.

I pick up the phone. "Hi, Otto, how are you doing?"

Otto responded, "Okay…I guess…"

"What's that mean? I hear something in your voice. Tell me what's wrong."

"It's probably nothing. But…I feel funny, something in my chest, perhaps I'm getting a cold." Otto sloughed it off.

"What do you mean, something in your chest? What does it feel like?"

"Oh, it's been like that since yesterday, I feel sort of full. Some pressure."

"Since *yesterday*!?! Why didn't you say anything this morning?"

"I didn't want to worry you."

"Great. Well, you've certainly got my attention now. Did you call the doctor?"

"Yes, he told me to call 911."

I took a deep breath, and said with forced humor, "Otto… so you think I'm 911? Stay on the line. I'll call 911 from here. Wait until I get to another phone in the office. Don't hang up!"

This was before cell phones. *The only clear thing going through my head was that this was taking way too long, and I really needed to get him to a hospital… and I was twenty-three miles away… and it felt like we were talking under water… and time was racing both too fast and dragging too slowly.*

Otto shouted into the phone, "NO! If an ambulance comes, I'm not getting in it! Dr. K. is only at Skokie Valley Hospital today, and I'm not going anywhere except there! He is the only one I trust! An ambulance will take me to the nearest hospital, and that is probably way west of here, and I'm NOT GOING!"

Good grief, Charlie Brown. *Now what do I do? Please, oh please, let me call this right.* He had become so excited that I decided it was best to try to keep him calm. My mind flashed back to only a few months before. At that time Otto needed two four-pronged canes, to walk safely. He'd lost his balance, then fell, wedging himself between the concrete wall and his car in our tiny garage. He could still drive then, and when he didn't keep his appointment for physical therapy, they called me, and I called the paramedics. When the paramedics found him, he insisted they place him in his lift chair, and not transport him to the hospital. I couldn't believe they listened to him! Otto was always extremely persuasive, even when down and almost counted out. I feared he'd do the same thing this time, without me there. I told him I'd leave right away, and get him to Skokie Valley Hospital. I drove like a crazy person, with as much safety as possible, while going as fast as possible, all the way to Buffalo Grove. I loaded him into the car, turned around, and drove back to the Skokie hospital, because he didn't want to go anywhere else.

Upon arriving at the hospital, when I mentioned a possible heart attack, they admitted him immediately to an emergency room. Those were the days when I was asked to step out for a minute, while they hooked him up to the monitoring devices. I had barely reached the waiting room, when the admitting male nurse reached me, and urgently asked me to return to the examining room.

Guess what? Otto was refusing any treatment by anyone. He wouldn't even let them put the EKG tabs on him until his doctor arrived to the ER! Our doctor was in surgery, and not available for a while. I asked the nurse to step out for a minute. I leaned in very close to Otto's ear, and in that soft, low tone I reserved for absolutely desperate situations—we'd been through many by this time—I told him I would walk out of the hospital immediately, and leave him there by himself, to fend off the entire hospital staff, alone.

He hesitated briefly, checking the look on my face. I had put on my 'toughest tough', practiced over many years dealing with resistant students, and he relented, quietly ready for the worst. I called the nurse in from the hall, and told him Otto was ready now. When the nurse affixed the final pad to his chest, he blurted out, "Yes, he's having a heart attack, right now, as we speak."

I think one of the hardest things to manage when handling loved ones' medical issues—especially with long-term disability and the steady spiral of diminishing mental or physical capacities—is determining the exact amount and the precise timing of appropriate intervention. How do you preserve the patient's dignity and independence? Those must always be weighed against the advised medical procedures. Sometimes it's a guessing game, sometimes it's prayer.

Tightrope walking is a well-practiced art of the caretaker. Too bad that special umbrella for balance kept hiding in the closet many days, hoping it wouldn't be needed again.

50-50

What is the rest of that story? How did it go? How serious was Otto's heart attack in 1988? It started with three weeks in the Skokie hospital in Cardiac Intensive Care for a while, followed by enough improvement to move him 'up' to regular Cardiac Care. Consults with his medical staff always ended with question marks on our family's and doctors' foreheads. Surgery was ruled to be far too dangerous for Otto's complex bank of medical needs. Keeping his heart stable—with its newly diagnosed non-functioning areas of muscle and arterial blockages—was a losing battle at this point.

When he 'coded' for a third time, near the end of the third week, staff did an about-face regarding bypass not being a viable option. I heard the code signal announced as I was heading to his room after eating lunch, and when I saw the crash cart outside his room, all my hope faded. For the past three weeks, the doctors had refused to recommend him for heart bypass—a procedure in its early stages then—because of his many illnesses: multiple sclerosis, diabetes, and COPD. But with this third heart stoppage, they had no more miracles, and he would be transferred to St. Francis in Evanston, which had just started doing bypasses, in this brave new heart-remedy world of the late 1980s.

At St. Francis Hospital, a few family members and I quickly learned our way through the labyrinth of entries and floors. We gathered in his room at the end of that transfer day, waiting to meet the surgeon. In talking with the doctor at Skokie Valley, we requested that Otto be given the most experienced doctor to perform the surgery. Otto's cardiologist said he would see what he could do, but made no promises. The evening of admittance, we waited for the surgeon to come brief us. Surgery was quickly scheduled for the following day, due to the seriousness of Otto's problems. There were two physicians doing bypasses at that time. I hoped either would be fine. Dr. S. walked into Otto's room, greeted us with a serious, competent look, and quickly gave Otto the good news, followed by the bad news, as we all held our breath in resigned silence.

The good news? The surgeon was willing to perform the surgery. The bad news? He stated that heart bypass had not, to that point, been performed successfully on anyone with as many serious diseases as Otto, and that he had only a 50% chance of survival. None of the family dared to look at each other, as we all understood that 50-50 chance dashed our hopes of any good odds for success.

However, Otto's face lit up. He smiled broadly for the first time in several days, clasped the doctor's hand and thanked him profusely! I clearly remember signaling a slight shake of my head to the doctor, hoping he would grasp my meaning, and would NOT explain to Otto what 50% meant. He looked a little quizzical, but hid his doubt from all of us, and made no further attempt to explain the seriousness of the operation to Otto. It was at that moment I was so thankful that somewhere in the many years of tortured living and hiding in Europe, perhaps Otto's math instruction had been minimal, and eliminated his fear at this crucial point in his life. Maybe he *added* those two 50s, and got 100%!

Somehow, but definitely odd for a family that talks nonstop—and loves to correct anyone else's mistakes—just this one important time, no one spoke. Amazing!

We gathered around a large table in the waiting room early the following morning. Again, we were much quieter than usual, with only small talk—and, of course, buckets of unspoken thoughts—filling those interminable hours which ticked along slowly.

At last, I was able to go into the recovery area—into the coldest room I'd ever felt indoors—for a few moments, to see Otto, looking so pale, hooked to numerous pieces of tubing and machines. We each took quick turns, and one by one we came back to the waiting room, trying not to pre-condition the others with any fear of what we had just observed. I was a little worried that when I was in with Otto, he appeared to be anxious, even though sedated, and a frown lingered on his forehead. I mentioned this to the family when I returned to the waiting room.

When our daughter, Michelle, took her turn, she went in for the requisite couple of minutes, and when she came out, she was laughing! My first thought was *how inappropriate*. The tension of her dad's illness and surgery must have taken its toll, and I attributed her smiles to the nervousness we all felt. However, she quickly explained her reason for laughing. When she entered the recovery room, she said some encouraging thoughts to her dad. Then he seemed to gesture to her, with his eyes and eyebrows. They were all he could move. She assessed the situation, and somehow figured out what he needed.

She said, "It's okay, Dad, you can go right ahead…just pee into the tube! You are all hooked up!"

Apparently, he did. He managed to smile a thanks to her with his eyes.

We all relaxed for the first time in many weeks!

Finally, the surgeon came out to speak to us, informing us that all had gone fairly well, and the next few days would be key to determining success or failure. As he left, he pulled me aside and whispered to me that it was the most unusual heart bypass (quadruple) he had performed to date. Then he stopped. I said, "Why?"

"Because…it was as if I was not in control of the instruments. It was as if someone, something…was guiding them, moving them just so." He became very quiet again. I cannot convey the amount of joy his words brought to me. This physician had an ascetic air that seemed to float around him, and when you were in his presence, you knew you were at peace, and that whatever could be done, had been done, in the best way, with skill and reverence. For your very loved, loved one. Otto gained fifteen more years of living from that skill. Thank you.

The DNA of DNR

Bring that memory back one more time. Medical management—including pharmaceutical decisions, treatment decisions, and all that weighs in on the patient and the caretaker—creates a narrow and fragile scaffold walkway that must be negotiated with great care, using all you know to get across that shallow ice to keep the patient as healthy as possible and avoid any mishaps.

Each day is a challenge. All of the many hospitalizations following a surgery, trauma, infection, or pneumonia carried new puzzles that needed solving. They had common threads, but each had its own minefield, minus a GPS to guide us. But play the game we did. Late in the game, we almost failed.

One particular hospitalization wasn't going well. Otto's systems didn't respond to any treatment. He was hospitalized for several days, but his ability to transfer or regain even limited mobility seemed to have diminished greatly. His spirits were down. I knew we were going to need new rehabilitation therapies in order to eventually be able to take him home.

At this point he would require home help in the daytime, while I still needed to work full time. In the past two years we had managed to adapt to his downturns in strength and provide enough support in order to make him safe at home. I hoped we could do it again, but I was much less sure this time.

The year was 2001, and sixteen years had gone by since Otto had to stop working, the last twelve of them requiring him to use one cane, then two canes, then two canes with four rubber prongs attached; and finally, a wheelchair, followed by an elaborate four-wheeled electric scooter. Safe transfers were mandatory if he was to maintain by himself at home during hours I was out working. I was becoming less able to lift him for transfers, and this time we had hit a wall. Both of us.

Neither of us said that aloud, of course, but we both knew it.

Over the years of health issues and hospitalizations, I had become familiar with his medical needs, and while I was probably an annoyance for the doctors, I had learned to investigate, resource, and be very present in mind and body for every treatment and medication. I give myself an 'A' in advocacy. I have only praise and thanks for his doctor who saw him through those eighteen years, as I know Otto wouldn't have made it without him.

I entered the hospital as usual that night and asked for his chart. I began doing this on a regular basis a year before, so I would know who had attended him while I was working, and I could check on treatments and medications. Believe me, I know how the staff nurses must have resented me, and probably wished I were not so nosy. My desire to stay on top of it all trumped my desire to avoid irritating the nurses or doctors. Throughout Otto's many hospitalizations, there were several mistakes that happened—some inconsequential, some dangerous. Reading the daily chart helped me stay on top of things. That night I sat in the hall outside Otto's room and set the large (by this time, very thick) chart down on my lap.

Red. R-E-D! Bold red letters at the top of his chart.

I couldn't believe my eyes. Shaking and stunned, I read the letters again. "DNR". Do Not Resuscitate! *Stop, Sarah… think… this can't be happening.*

I looked again. No mistake. "DNR."

I took several deep breaths, thoughts racing, stood up, walked to the nurse at the desk, and with my most quiet and measured voice—covering up my raging, unquiet emotions laced with terror—I asked, "What do these letters mean on my husband's chart? They certainly weren't there yesterday."

The nurse calmly explained what I already suspected. "DNR means: Do Not Resuscitate." I've experienced long minutes before, but I am sure this was the longest I had ever waited to ask a question of such extreme importance. "Can you please get the doctor who wrote this on the chart… on the phone? Now."

He answered her immediately, thank heaven.

"Why is there a DNR on Otto's chart?" I asked. I wanted to shout it, but I clenched my teeth and kept hold of my anger.

"I spoke with Otto this afternoon," he replied.

Breathe, Sarah.

"And? What did you talk about?" I tried to stay calm. I wanted the answer desperately. I didn't want the answer that seemed likely to be forthcoming.

"Well… he said he didn't want to live this way," the doctor responded.

I was stunned. My head filled with desperate questions.

Otto, the survivor. The survivor of city-to-city escapes, the survivor of repeated captures, the survivor on little food… just scraps for so many years. The survivor of final capture. The survivor of Dachau… THAT survivor would never say he is giving up! What has happened? What's different? What do I do now?

I thanked the doctor and hung up, taking a few minutes to think things through and compose myself before going into Otto's room. I have always held a firm belief that each person has the right to determine his physical and mental limits. I believed I needed to support Otto in his desires, even if they were contrary to my need to keep him alive. It would be selfish of me to do that, if he could no longer handle the steadily diminishing quality of his life.

However, I needed to know what he had said. Even though I risked upsetting him if he did not want me to know he had requested *not* to be revived, I needed to know for certain that *this was his own request,* before I could go along with it. A tiny part of me still held out hope that this was all a mistake, and hadn't really happened. I started with small talk.

"So-o-o, Otto, what's new? How was your day?" I asked, looking at him carefully, checking his mood, his eyes, his lips, for any hint of his feelings. Nothing stood out as different.

We chatted a little. He told me what he had for lunch. I told me what had happened in school that day. Finally, I said, "Did anybody visit you today? What doctors did you see?"

"The usual," he replied.

"Did our favorite doctor come in?"

"Yes, yes he did."

"Good. What did you talk about?"

"I asked him how I was doing, and what was he thinking to give me to make me better," he replied. A small glimmer of hope flickered through me.

"Can you remember exactly what you said?"

One of the things I loved most about Otto was that he had always been really good at telling me whole conversations about his day and he had a memory for details that made you feel like you were there. I am an umbrella thinker…Otto always recounted every raindrop. Please let him remember this one!

Otto thought for a minute.

"Yes…we talked a while, and then he got sort of quiet. Then he asked me if I wanted to live this way."

Here it comes. I thought I would faint, but I needed to know. "And, what did you say to him?"

"I said no, of course not!"

I lost all hope. It was as I had feared. He no longer wanted to live.

Weary, but resigned, I clutched at one more frantic thought, and asked, "What did you mean by that, Otto?"

"What do you think I meant?" Otto replied. "I meant he should get me well quickly, and get me out of here!"

Otto had no idea why I burst out laughing and crying simultaneously that day. I had the answer I needed. I had the answer I so desperately wanted. He was Otto. He was my Otto. He was my survivor. He was my hero. And, as always, his wonderful doctor continued to be my hero, also. I called him. He removed the DNR from Otto's chart.

November 22, 1963
The Day History Came Live

As I write this memory, it is November of 2013, fifty years since that horrible day. In 1963, I was almost 25, Otto was 34. We lived in Chicago, a small garden-basement apartment on Briar Place, off Sheridan. Leigha, our oldest daughter, was two. I had received my B.A. degree in August, and began to work as an FTB (full time basis) substitute in the Chicago Public Schools, teaching eighth-grade science on the north side of town. Our world was right side up.

Leigha was a delightful young lady who filled us with joy. It was a time of bright hope and it seemed like many productive and happy years stretched ahead of us. For those in our twenties, the young family in the White House was so close to us in age—closer than any politicians prior to this—that they became part of our lives. We saw them almost as a personal link to the world and its events. Television brought them into our homes. For women, the prominence and strength of Jacqueline Kennedy created our own role model for a strong female presence, and that mirrored the growing feminine psyche that supported women in our quest for equal opportunity and recognition.

And then that shot rang out.

In one second our world fell apart.

Everyone remembers that day. I had just completed my lunch period at school. My eighth-grade students straggled in from their homes. Chicago children at that time attended school in their immediate neighborhoods and went home for lunch. Staff had been informed of the shooting of President Kennedy during the lunch period. As my students entered, some of them knew of the shooting, but they didn't appear to be very affected by it at this time. As the news of our President's death was announced, a quiet shock and sadness permeated the afternoon. As always, teachers serve to maintain stability in the face of tragedy. Years later, on September 11, 2001, I would again experience the futility of trying to translate death and insanity to a young middle-grade class in Mundelein, Illinois.

That 1963 weekend was devoted to our family, with moments for catching the horrible scenes on the television. These were the days of only one TV in most households, and I am so thankful that we didn't have one on throughout the whole day in each room of the apartment. The images were stunning. My childhood did not include strong visuals in the home setting. Only at arm's length did I ever view even mild horror, at occasional movies in theaters, with those movies being *Wizard of Oz* types, not real-life drama, and definitely not murder. Death didn't play in our homes. Newsreels on theater movie screens showed only rare glimpses, mostly of wars far across an ocean. Chaos was held at a safe distance and seemed much further away than a movie screen. I had no trouble *reading* Edgar Allen Poe. I have never been able to *watch* even one minute of a horror film.

Fifty years of the world's evils displayed at arm's length through television, and today on our cell phones, make it seem like we always had that up close and personal access. Yet I know the resulting coverage of the assassination and its aftermath, including the live filming of the shooting of Lee Oswald by Jack Ruby, marked the beginning of live reporting on television, unfiltered and immediate. I am fairly certain I happened to be watching the television at the moment of Oswald's shooting. It also could be that it was aired so many times that I felt I was there, but wasn't. Virtual or real memory? Horrible either way.

Otto and I had met and married in 1960. Otto faced extreme evil and devastation as a Jewish survivor of the Holocaust, with multiple moves from city to city and many captures and life-threatening dangers. From the time he was nine or ten until he was liberated at sixteen, extending into his later teens in the aftermath, he lost his father and so many family members. His mother and brother survived. I remember one discussion thread that ran throughout our marriage—a topic we never could agree on.

I argued that the lessons learned by humanity, resulting from the devastation in World War II, would continue to guide us, and civilization would move forward, wiser and more humane. Our discussion always ended in a stalemate. Otto would always say, his vehement assertion backed up with his horrible first-hand experience, "It will happen again."

All through our forty-three years together, I responded with, "No, we've learned our lesson. People won't be that evil ever again."

Otto had faith in the goodness of some. He had equally strong faith in the ignorance of others, and some peoples' capacity to do evil and follow leaders who encourage evil. I am so sorry that, as of this writing, it seems Otto has been proven right and I was wrong.

176 First Days of School

One hundred seventy-six days of attendance is the average length of a public-school year in Illinois. Each day seemed like a 'first day', that year; there were no two the same. I should have known what the 1969-70 school year was going to bring as I sat with seventy teachers in the spotless lunchroom of Schiller School in Chicago. It was my first full-time teaching position. I had over an hour's commute each way, with three children, Leigha, Michael, and Michelle, ages two, four, and almost eight, waiting for me at home each night. The Cubs were completing their best year in my lifetime. What could go wrong?

As stacks of new school year teacher orientation papers fluttered down the table rows, I sat back in quiet anticipation. I have always felt comfortable in a school setting. Feeling appropriately dressed in my sedate and proper schoolmarm garb, I glanced around to see my fellow teachers looking attentive. What did I notice in that first glance? Most of us were young—there didn't seem to be many faces over forty. Odd. I was to learn that the more challenging schools in the system could become a temporary turnstile for more experienced staff who sought transfers. After a few years of service, teachers could put their names on transfer lists and move to schools that were less crowded, more stable, closer to home, and therefore, maybe better options for a long career.

As I listened to the hum of two woefully inadequate floor fans at the far back corners of the cafeteria, I became lulled by the drone of the principal and his two assistants while they listed their important goals—which sounded more like demands—for the year. Until I sat up suddenly—wide awake at the end of that one message from the principal, as he tied off the meeting.

"Now hear me, hear me loud and clear. Get this straight, from now until June. The office is not here for your problems. I am not here for your problems. And, I warn you. You will have problems. Deal with them as best you can. Talk with your teammates. Find a teacher friend near you. When you have exhausted any and all solutions, then and only then, consult one of the assistant principals. I am far too busy to hold so many hands."

The threatening branding of his hands-off support system—asked for, but not going to be forthcoming—seared this message in my mind and remains there to this day.

Woefully inadequate. The term that I had applied to the floor fans breezed again through my mind. This time I assigned it to the principal's speech.

Lesson #1: "You're on your own." I heard it loud and clear. Little did I know the extent of the inadequacy. Little did I know the extent of my own shortcomings.

It was a page-turner year.

Pages two through one hundred seventy-six unfolded quickly, with action on every one. My teacher preparation, my couple of years of teaching in part-time and substitute positions in Chicago and Milwaukee, my passion and compassion—all would be tested. Many days I would be found lacking. There were weeks I prayed for at least a D+ on those tests.

I spent some time trying to pump up my spirits before I visited my classroom. What could be easier than having a fifth-grade class for my first full year of teaching? Kids ten or eleven years old. I can certainly handle this, I thought to myself. When we were released from our first day of indoctrination in the lunchroom, I climbed the flights of stairs to my classroom, excited for the first view of my daytime home for the next nine months.

Using the key provided, remembering the admonition to KEEP THE DOOR LOCKED AT ALL TIMES, EVEN WHEN YOU ARE IN THE ROOM—I turned the key in the lock, and swiveled around to case the joint.

NO! THIS CAN'T BE. I felt like I had been hit in the gut with a ninety-mile-an-hour curve ball. The entire window wall 'wasn't'! The window wall was made of hastily affixed wooden planks where the window glass should have been. All except for the one closest to the front of the room. That lone window was free of boards and retained its window glass, which served as the sole source of natural light to the room. *Deep breath here.* Walk around the room, check the desks and chairs. Not bad. Seemed to be a lot of them, so at first, I didn't notice what was missing in the classroom.

There were no other pieces of furniture. No bookcases. No books to line their shelves. Surely, they would arrive before tomorrow's start? I was still an optimist at that point. Need I say that no books ever arrived that year? Books, I was told, were useless here. Instruction was designed for a unified presentation by 'experienced' teachers on the one lonely television screen in the room, to make certain all students in the school learned the same content. I assume central office instructors were filmed. They provided some of the most boring and meaningless lessons I would ever be responsible for. My job was to roam the rows, pretending to convince these children that what they saw was grand.

It was obvious that the philosophy behind this unified instructional method was to ensure a core of learning that would reach all children, regardless of the variety of teachers in the building, or the inexperience of newer staff. Did it work?

Of course not.

The second reason books were taboo was that it was believed if sent home for homework, they would never return. It would therefore be a waste to provide them. *Absurd.*

I felt like Teacher Alice, down the rabbit hole. Nothing made sense in that setting on that first day. I knew instantly that I was going to need to dispense with everything I had been taught about classroom instruction. I felt I should throw my own 'teaching book' out that single open window the first day...

Remember the 'keep-it-locked' direction, Lesson #2? The reason you were to lock the classroom door was so the class would be safe from intruders in the hall. However, the contradictory admonition was, "If it appears that a gang member is standing at your door and wants to come in, then you are to let him."

WHAT? Yes, right. We were to let him in. Because if we didn't, he was likely to shoot the door open, and we wouldn't want that to happen, now would we?

Opening day, enter the fifth graders. I wish I could tell you how wondrous that first day of meeting and greeting was. I wish I remembered each detail, and the details of the awesome lesson I prepared to engage them and kick off the year.

I don't remember.

Let's just say they and I got through that first day. I taught. Some of them listened. Many of them had built up several years of practiced resistance under their belts. But then I had a couple of decades of stubborn attitude under my belt, or so I've been told.

The first giant hurdle to overcome was the range of ages. It was a fifth-grade classroom. I had children from eleven to sixteen years old! This possibility was never mentioned in any teacher-training courses. Nor was it mentioned on our workshop day. I suppose the plan was to group this particular class at a unified academic performance level of one to two years below fifth-grade ability. The flaw in this plan was the accumulated learning and behavioral issues the kids had gathered along their way. Another glitch was the tendency to provide separate (pullout) support for kids with severe behavioral issues only for the *second* half of each year. Each fall, they would be placed back into regular classes, even if they had not made measurable progress, to see if they could 'make it on their own'.

Guess what? It didn't work. Shades of Sisyphus. Each new teacher spent the first half of every year building the behavior documentation that would earn that student the smaller classroom and specialized support he should have been entitled to in the first place, from the first day in September. This half-in, half-out, limp-along philosophy provided a continuity of failure, rather than targeted and continuous support.

Existing on slim bits of hope and advice from my coworker mentors, along with a true knight— Jesse White, the gym teacher (for many years now, our fine Illinois Secretary of State) —I began to build a breadcrumb path through this forest of failure. Three months into the school year, I had changed greatly. I was thirty pounds lighter (not by choice—by stress), and I was 'becoming' a good teacher. Why? Because I stopped trying to bring everyone up to *someone else's* expectation dot, placed on a test-data tracking sheet.

I designed my own learning curve for each child, starting with where he was, not where he should be. Looking back now, I think that as the year progressed, my students noticed I was real, I was concerned, I was on their side, and they felt I could be trusted to lead them toward success.

Each day wasn't perfect. In the winter months, I never did manage to get my students to leave their coats on the hooks in the cloakroom area on our inside wall. It was open for all to see, in case anyone tried to take something from a pocket, but they protected their possessions and didn't even trust the hooks on the wall, ten feet away. Maybe wearing their coats helped them feel more secure. I relinquished that argument, picking the battles that would help a student grow.

I never grew accustomed to such experiences as having a student's slightly older brother chew me out on Parent Conference Day, for placing a 'D' on a report card. I definitely learned to be thrilled that any family member took the time to show up. I learned to smile warmly on the outside, though I needed to scream on the inside some days.

A major turning point came on the day I was told one of the students had a handmade gun in his possession. I had no choice but to confront him in the classroom, as he arrived for the day. I have no memory of his features. I do remember he was of average height for a fifth grader, and he had not presented any problems in the classroom up to that day. Later on, if I had to pin a reason on his 'concealed carry' that morning, I would guess he had brought the gun to school as a measure of protection, rather than a threat to others. However, attempting to remove it might cause a dangerous confrontation. No choice but to try. These strategies raced through my mind.

Eye contact. Steady gaze.
Hand extended. Few words.
Don't show you are quivering.
Bluff your way through it.
Don't look away for a second.
Don't show FEAR.
PRAY. PRAY. PRAY.

And…he handed it over. I remembered that 'loud and clear' message from the first day of the year, "handle your own problems, don't expect help from me, I'm far too busy." I handled that gun problem. I had never touched a gun prior to that day. Thank heaven I have not had to touch one since.

I noticed a new respect traveled through my classroom. I think it had a lot to do with the kids feeling I could protect them. I wasn't flighty. I wasn't crazy. I wasn't scared. *Little did they know.* I lived in the boat with them. I wasn't going to tip us over.

⁂

I can't leave that Schiller schoolyear without two more challenging examples. Remember the 'gang member at the door' rule, on Day One?

Slight knock on the door window. I looked up to see a young man. Casual clothes. I was aware that I had been provided a list somewhere of the combination of colors belonging to various gangs. I had never wanted to memorize it, or even to think about it. I don't think it would have helped me in this situation. Would I have done anything differently, even if I had known to which gang he belonged? I walked to the door and opened it, with my better judgment hopping up and down wildly in my brain, saying *NO! NO! NO!*

"Jus' wanna talk with the kids for a minute, Teach."

"Now's not a good time…we're doing a hard math lesson. Could you come back later?" *Worth a try.*

"Nah, now's the best time for me. I ain't got all day."

I made a quick check to see if I saw any weapons. None apparent. I let him into the room. He immediately took his place in front of my desk, facing the class. It was a calm speech. Friendly sounding. He told the kids he was their friend. He told them he was the person to go to if they were in trouble. He gave them an address. He did not identify the name of the 'group'. He said things worked better in the community if he and his 'members' had helpers. He again promised protection.

Short and sweet.

Short. Threatening.

After he left, I decided against any debriefing class discussion of the incident. The chance that he was a relative or friend of one of the class members was probably high. My need for caution, to prevent any word getting back to him, outweighed my teacher instinct to help the students process the situation. I reported it to the office as soon as I had a break. I am sure nothing was 'done'.

Then there was the day of the fire. My mind echoed *this is not a drill, this is the real thing.* My class and I were on the third floor of the school. We could smell the smoke before the alarm clanged. The halls and stairwells were filling up fast with the haze. When the fire alarm went off, we moved fast. I told students to crouch as low as possible and move quickly down the several flights of steps, then out the back door to the playground. I remember thinking we were accomplishing such an orderly exit. While chaos would have been warranted, this large number of kids knew it was for real and they needed to move quickly and maintain order.

And that's just what we tried to do. For several hours. Hundreds of students and staff stood or sat in fairly straight lines on our asphalt playground. We didn't dismiss until the end of the day when the final bell rang. We couldn't re-enter the building because of the lingering smoke, even though the fire had been successfully put out.

Why didn't we send the kids home early? Easy. They couldn't be sent home to the 'projects' until the end of the day, because if parents weren't home to receive them, the school would be responsible for their safety during regular school hours.

Oh, and what was the fire all about? A student had managed to enter the teacher lounge-workroom on the second floor, grab the mimeo machine fluid, sprinkle it about and light it. A heroic janitor saved the building and limited the damage to property and other people, hurting himself in the process.

Days rolled into more days, until they added up to 176. Just another year in a school in the projects. What did I learn? I learned I could teach anyone, anything, anywhere—under the most adverse circumstances. I learned that no matter how strong I would become as a teacher, I would never have the strength of any one of those kids—they had to survive that life, day and night. I drove home each day at 3:30.

Once You Start Hydroplaning, You Need to Get a Grip

D ry pavement, Thanksgiving Day, November 1954. I was fifteen years old. My brother, Chuck, twelve years older, relented to my plea to let me take over the wheel on the way back to our Thanksgiving dinner at his house. He was a soft touch for a quick practice drive on Fremont Street, after we went home to retrieve the forgotten fruit salad.

When I missed the U-turn at the end of the block, Chuck laughed, and I felt a faint coming on, but held it together. I had almost made the curve. The salad didn't. Our twenty fingers picked up what they could from the floor-mat, and frantically re-arranged the fruit back in the bowl. No salad belts back in the day! Lesson: Invent seat belts for salads...you never know when they'll come in handy.

Setting: a Dubuque slumber party late-night sneak-out drive, to prove we were all grown up, and didn't need anyone to help us. Sixteen years old, 1955. Four or five girlfriends. Country road not too far out of town. Almost made that curve, too. Knocked on farmhouse door after walking back up the road. Kindly farmer and his tractor pulled our car from the ditch that warm night. We never heard a word from our parents. Thank heavens the farmer in the dell didn't tell! Lesson: Perhaps we still needed help, after all.

❧

Northwest Iowa. Mid-winter snowstorm, 1958-1959. College roommate's wedding. Nineteen years old. Two-lane road edges obscured. Slippery. Driving carefully, not too fast. The scene would have made a great slow-motion camera shot, as the tires locked in a skid and we skittered sideways on the highway, then down the gentle embankment, finally landing stalled in the ditch. Still not grown up. Lucky there was little traffic on the road that day. Unlucky that it took a while for someone to come along and offer help. Passersby observed our predicament and drove us out, after checking that our tires seemed okay. Missed the ceremony. Made the reception. Lesson: Old enough to get married, not old enough to drive in snow.

❧

Early evening, September 6, 2013. My daughter, Michelle, her husband, Steve, two of their children, Max and Maya, and I drove in two cars as we were returning home to Grayslake, following a fun Labor Day party at my daughter Leigha's home in Evanston. Grandson Max is almost sixteen years old. The busy end of Labor Day traffic moved north, above Lake Street on Route 41 at a fast pace. Suddenly, up ahead, cars scatter. Michelle pulls off to the right, and parks near a bridge and a steep embankment, at the side of the tollway. The skidding car has come to rest upside down. Smoke rises. Max, before the car stops, throws open his door and races down the embankment in his flip-flops, along with a man from another car, and Michelle and Steve. Together, they pull open the door and carefully remove an injured young woman from the passenger seat. The driver is in shock, but mumbles that their baby is still in the car. Michelle keeps the gasping mother's head and neck stable in her lap, as Max and his dad make another run to rescue the baby from the rear of the car, safely strapped into a car seat. Lessons: Things happen quickly, assess and act quickly. There is no age requirement for a hero.

Words, Words, Words

I THINK IT STARTED WITH those flash cards with all the new words on them. The words I was taught and those I taught my classes always held a deep lifelong fascination for me. Every time a new flashcard word filled up my brain's RAM, I tried to file them all away and use them in future communication. How silly of me. Of course, that's an impossible task. Like my belief in the Tooth Fairy, it is a figment of imagination. A wishful dream similar to thinking I can read all the classics, or that I will reach that one hoped-for day not too far in the future when all the clutter in my closets will organize itself, before I am forced to appear on one of those home hoarders shows. Feeling like I have run out of my personal memory capacity exactly two years ago, I now realize that my dream of gathering and retaining all the necessary words is just a fantasy.

From 'A' to Me

It probably started on that day that occupies only one brief scene in my mind, no details, no prologue, no next step—just a slight memory of being hit on my nose by a girl in my kindergarten class. Imagine that, in those good old days. Not just hit on my nose, but hit with a dictionary! I count my blessings that the dictionaries were smaller in 1944, but somewhat heavy, nonetheless. Yes, that's likely where my passion for words started. There has always been a raised part on the bridge of my nose, not especially prominent, yet still there.

I think my brain became filled with all those words, and I wanted even more of them to be absorbed, hopefully in a much safer way. From that day on, which closely coincided with learning to read, I read nonstop, living in each author's reality, traveling around the world in word ships, with character sail-mates at my side.

"Keep reading" is what I said to each child I taught, because I valued the deep pleasure that great authors brought to my own life. In the past few years I have watched the large bookstores overtake the small cozy ones. I saw the writing on the wall. Next, I watched that large bookstore overtaken by the economy and technological change of reading and information gathering habits. It was hard not to smile that its size deserved it.

Yet each of these losses speaks of gigantic shifts in how we behave and learn. Will a generation from now be so impacted with tweet-length communication that our human patience and time set aside to read large books will be gone forever? And, in the production end, will the massive change to self-publishing, sound bites, and 280-character celebrity and not-so-celebrity Tweet epiphanies eliminate any general, thoughtful, coordinated, or measured literate advancement of ideas and thought, and reliable news? Hold out, humanity. Hold out.

Which Words?

The ones spoken
in anger,
preferably in delight.
They float
or bump
or fight.
Fraught with fright
and, "No,
that's-not-what-I-meant."

Noun fists bump together in the air
seeking arousal or hurt,
or hopefully,
just
understanding.
Perhaps a minimal response,
or a full friendly hand held out to greet.
Just hanging there.
Colorful ornaments or useful clothes hooks?
Spinning light to dark shades of meaning.

I Suffer from Bifocal Blurbs

They can't be serious. There are 7,643,231 teeny-tiny minced words on that page. Bifocal blurbs that disclaim responsibility for causing bodily symptoms that definitely suggest alien takeover. This is modern science? How dense do they think I am?

Ask my doctor? If he has the time to read through all of these prescription precautions and then research them, how can he be keeping up with the really great new methods of treating my diseases?

I guess I'm just supposed to skim it, feel uplifted and positive that white-coated researchers can string fifty-two Latin prefixes to one hundred twenty-nine bases, and then add twenty-seven suffixes to describe what I certainly *don't* want to experience, along with my current illness.

My Prescription Label Warning: "Do not read, do not buy, and above all, do not open or ingest. Turn the page to find out how to thrill your loved one, lose twenty-eight pounds overnight, cook better than your mother-in-law, and turn cellulite into celery. Just beware of all the aforementioned calamities that may befall you! Remember, we warned you, so don't even think of coming back to us if your left pinky fingernail turns bright purple and falls off!"

Yes, that's it. This prescription is fantastic! *I think I am feeling better already. Yes. Yes, indeed. I know I am better!* I don't need this pill. Its threat is effective, all by itself. The strength of words.

Looking for Just
the Write Word

There is no other word for it. No better word to describe the brazen impertinence of my writer's ego.

How dare I believe for even an instant that after all the important writings through the ages, my writings need to be written? Those on the stone tablets carried up the Mount. Those in cuneiform indentations on the Rosetta stone. Those written in scarlet on a downtrodden woman's chest by a holier-than-thou finger pointer. . .

But I digress. How is it possible that each time I approach my keyboard, I still believe I have something to say, something to create?

How can someone who still believes a tooth placed under her pillow will earn cash, be considered a writer of worth? How can someone who searches for a yellow brick road to lead her to a wizard willing to teleport her (after all, I am modern) back to Kansas, be a believable reporter? Can I really trust that gal who checks the closet each night, to see that all twenty-nine members of her Smurf collection are safely tucked in on the third shelf? How can that someone be of worth to place words of value on paper?

Chutzpah. That is the only possible answer. Chutzpah. Merriam Webster's first phrase defines chutzpah as "shameless boldness." Perfect. That's a fit! Without chutzpah, I could not even lift my finger to type the first word. Without chutzpah, I must suspend belief even when I write non-fiction. Without chutzpah, I couldn't show up to Critique Group, week after week, seeking absolution. Oops! Did I say that?

Speech Lesson: To correctly pronounce a Hebrew or Yiddish 'ch' sound, one must use more than just the tongue and lips. It goes deeper than that. It requires a guttural, back-of-the-throat closing, with some gurgle-y waterfall faucet involvement. Feels like you have a large piece of matzo stuck in the back of your throat, and you need to politely clear it before you choke.

Back to my story. There I am, at the computer, coffee on my right side, iPhone on my left. Keyboard dusted off. I have to be sure of the word. I thumb through the pages of my mind, checking. Armed with just enough cheekiness—no, not right.

Gall? No, not right.

Effrontery? Definitely no.

Arrogance? Lord, NO!

I prefer the Free Dictionary's simple definition of chutzpah—a Yiddish term meaning audacity, courage, or nerve. That's it! Chutzpah. A writer has to reach deep, way back in the throat, and cough up the courage to write. It's all in the guttural.

Contrasts

THIS SECTION POINTS TO THE connection between opposites, even between prose and poetry, often blending them in the same story. I fear that the revered English teachers of my earlier days at Dubuque Senior High School might approach, with their textbooks raised high in their hands, open to just the exact page that states, "Thou shalt *not* combine two literature forms in the same story," and all the other rules I have been so fond of breaking. Well, it just seems to work for me, and one of these stories 'wrote itself' in a combination of poetry and prose. So, yes, I'll take the 'B' instead of the 'A'. It's not always about the grades. (Please don't tell my mom that.)

Which One Is the Friend?

One
friend
always
nods
and
agrees with you.

One
friend
always
argues
and
questions.

My Sun Trumps Your Cloud

Your Cloud's Tears
Fall
Heavily
Earthward
Creating
Sad Rivers,
Deepening
Sorrow,
Drowning
My Light.

My Sun's Rays
Create
Warm Fuzzy Days
Leading to
Weightless,
Cool,
Comforting
Evenings on
Firefly Wings.

Inside, Outside

Inside,
I am a dancer
Light feet
Pointed toes
Graceful slides.

Outside,
Creaky knees
Slowed beat
Questioning steps
Timidly tread.

Focus
On the music,
Cha Cha Cha

Day Flakes, Night Flakes

Day snow
Troubles travelers
Binding highways
Icing byways.

Night snow
Windless falls
Dusting branches
Stars to earth
Sprinkling mirth.

Trackless Wonder
Snowman ready!

With Eyes Wide Open

One five-year-old, one three-year-old, and one nineteen-month toddler, with a tipsy red wagon headed downtown to Chicago, to view the decorated fiberglass cows in the *Cows on Parade* public art project. Their young mother and I walked along Michigan Avenue in August of 1999. We were fifty percent suburban sightseers, fifty percent *the sight*.

Chicago summers love the asphalt on Michigan Avenue. Chicago heat burrows deep down into the pavement, hugs it for a moment, then explodes back up to the worker and visitor populations with doubled force. And our beloved Lake Michigan enthusiastically releases its steam to create a sticky humid partner that makes the air each August particularly memorable.

It wasn't the longest walk I've ever taken. It just seemed so, as the day advanced.

Cows.
Cows everywhere,
Right side up, upside down.
Becca, the five-year-old, always says 'up-sa-lide-down'.

Facing north, south, east, in jest.
Some in pants, watch fob, and vest!
Pinks, blues, sequins, finery.
Artist whims in paint slick-shinery.
Most sustained the looks and touches
O'er months of visitors from far reaches,
Even Max!
And the nicest touch,
We heard Sami tell,
"Each one—and all— doesn't even smell!"

The first few blocks on the west side of Michigan Avenue stretched out quickly, corner to corner as we walked. We crossed to the east side and turned into the Tribune Plaza. We noticed we were slowing down. Stopping at each cow was shorter now, to match toddlers' interest, and the names of the creatures, penned in punny, funny words, were lost to those under four feet high. Rebecca, the five-year-old, began to notice the people instead of the sculptured cows. She was curious about what she saw. Her eyes lingered on the man with several bags hanging over his shoulders—old plastic bags, bags that certainly were not from any Michigan Avenue shops.

She saw a man sitting on the sidewalk with limbs fewer than hers. She saw the child in a wheelchair with arms in spasm. She became quiet. So quiet.

Sami and Max still watched the cows. Rebecca saw her known world changing. At first, her mom's brief answers to her questions sufficed. Then more was needed. The fun excursion changed to a life lesson, for this was more than Becca's little mind could absorb. So quickly. In a wagon. On a ninety-degree sunny August day, on Michigan Avenue in Chicago.

Then and Now

WHEN YOU REACH THE GRANDPARENT stage, your thoughts range from sitting squarely in today's moment to wandering backward to yesterday's minutes, triggered by simple bits of conversation or events happening so quickly now in front of you. You see those adorable grandkids standing tall and proud as they graduate from each level, just like your son and daughters did so few years ago. What a clever young person your granddaughter or grandson is when they tell you a delightful joke, just like your kids did. Wasn't that just last month? You grasp meaning from both the larger world screen and a kid's wagon view, in equal measure. Affected by all of it, limited in directing any of it, you hold your breath and hop on for the ride, praying that your loved ones safely catch that car right behind you, always wear their seatbelts, pack veggies in their lunch sacks, and turn in their homework.

These stories mark a few moments of worthwhile lessons, scattered over the years.

"Thanks, It's About Time"

I headed north on Milwaukee Avenue in Libertyville early this morning, August 11, 2015. As I approached the intersection of Milwaukee Avenue and Route 137, I noticed a square older-model pearl-white sedan ahead of me. Perched evenly spaced on the ledge above the rear seat, was a handsome array of United States Army caps, all with brims facing the same direction. They sat at full attention. I pictured the precision of a recruit's inspection-neat bunk area, and a parade march with each leg and arm moving in trained concert, in synchronized harmony. The license plate on the car identified a veteran, and Viet Nam as the battle theater.

It was time. Finally.

Checking all my mirrors, I couldn't resist quickly pulling around the right side of the car, into the curb lane, and matching its speed. I prayed all the traffic ahead of me and behind me would stay in its lane, so I could have just the right amount of space and safety for both our cars, to wave a high-five thumbs-up to the driver. In today's road-rage land, I feared he'd think I was offering him a different hand gesture for some perceived offense.

As I pulled forward and passed him on the right, I had just enough time to see his broad smile, and I hope he knew I was saying, "Thanks for your service!"

It was a long time coming.

It Does Take a Village

The first Parent-Teacher Conference Day at the beginning of the school year is always both eagerly awaited and dreaded. This year's directions indicate that parents are to visit the student's locker first, always a simple task at year's start. There are no ancient rotting-lunch 'science experiments' molding in the back corners yet. Yes, things look fine in here, gym shoes on the floor, toes facing the same way, jacket hanging over a hook. Two extra spiral notebooks sitting neatly on the top shelf, with the magnetic mirror only slightly askew on the inside of the locker door. It's amazing how that cyclonic transformation of a fifth grader's locker takes place over the next three months, ignoring parent and teacher admonitions to clean it once in a while. Locker neat? Check.

Next step in the process—read everything on the walls in the large double-class room, and compare granddaughter Sami's work to the other students. Papers on the wall look good? Check.

"I think we're ready to see your work area, Samantha," said my daughter, Michelle, Sami's mom. We all walked over to her desk. Did we detect a slowing down in Samantha's steps? Yes, there was definitely a reluctance on her part. She probably knew she had an 'A' on her locker neatness, judging by the smiles on our faces. Her hesitance now seemed to speak of a possible messy 'AHA' moment about to come, as we lifted the desk lid.

Yet, what should appear to our wondering eyes? A perfectly neat, artistically laid out, everything-in-its-place—Origami crane village! There, placed in awesome array, made out of carefully folded notebook paper, lived teeny, tiny cranes, in activity centers or at their miniature desks, in their little lift-the-lid classroom. There sat over one-hundred of them. Some cranes appeared to eat their lunches in a lunchroom area of the desk. They completed their schoolwork assignments, played in their playground area, and moved around their village each day, we imagined, as their designer busied herself during her classes, in her Queen of the Cranes desk domain! Was Samantha's school desk an example of neatness to the tenth degree? Check!

It was really hard to suppress our desire to burst out laughing with the grandest guffaws ever heard in school. I remember we were torn between praising Sami for her fabulous artwork and questioning her about her ability to stay focused during class. Her teachers always commented on her skills to construct anything, anyplace, and certainly at any time. Truer words were never spoken. We asked her to choose her time and place more wisely in the future. The crane village lived happily at home thereafter.

Nothing as It Was

Back up sixty or seventy years. Try to remember when you had to stand on tiptoes to reach forbidden fruits, especially those fresh-baked cookies you were told not to touch until after supper.

Think about all those excuses you devised to explain why you were late getting home, and there had to be a third call out the back door, then a fourth.

How clever you were to create numerous fictions to explain the mud on your little girl shoes in days when boys could play for hours in creek beds and their mud didn't warrant even a bare mention.

"Sarah Anne!"

Hear that? Yes, I still hear it today. Our first and middle names were used as a staccato signal that you were about to cross a rule line, and you'd better shape up or....

It was a time when kids seemed to live within a set of behavioral parentheses, to limit their infractions to moderation in all activities and interactions. Grownups stood at the top of all honored pyramids, while children squatted low-profile on the bottom, making sure they didn't bump into parents' patience.

I really looked forward to climbing that pyramid as I aged, to achieve adult status, to avoid being directed every second, to gain the automatic respect for just aging up to the top.

"Just you wait," I told myself as the years flew by.

But something happened on my way to age twenty-five. There was rebellion against the stiff formalities of child rearing. Psychologists advocated greater laissez-faire. Interest in Dr. Spock's rigid advice was traded in for the entertainment of a spike-eared Spock of the space fantasy *Star Trek*. Fun and games wedged out discipline and chores.

Child-centered rearing became the goal of parents bent on creating super kids, doing unto them what was not done unto the parents— supporting our psyches. Personally, I believe it was a necessary shift. However, our Silent Generation's conformist tendencies perhaps caused some of us to miss their 'shot'.

Silly-Con Valley
A Vocabulary Lesson

A funny thing happened on the way to critique-share this week. I needed to contact the WordPress techies for support help on a glitch on my website. They provide only online Chat service. Misnomer Alert! Chat refers to something warm and friendly, in one's leisure time. Do they realize the level of my blood pressure while I am trying to fix the unfixable, know the unknowable, ram the un-RAM-able?

If so, Chat would rename to Negotiation!

This type of support lengthens the time necessary to communicate an issue. You type. Then you wait. In what seems like five minutes, he types. You wait. His answer finally appears, and this choppy process goes on for an hour or more. A ten-minute live conversation would have solved my issue in a flash.

The good thing? I don't have to do this for a living. The other good thing? I have found that most of the techies have a sense of humor—if you insert some into this protracted conversation, they usually respond in kind. It makes the process more tolerable. I do have to weigh my need for 'instant' versus my need for a bit of fun to relieve the tension and monotony.

Yesterday's break in the solution action came when I had a lightbulb moment realizing that he had never really understood one of the three issues from the beginning. I decided to take the blame for not making it clear to him. I apologized, and said I would have to drink hemlock.

A couple of lines later, he responded that he was not familiar with hemlock, so he looked it up. He mentioned that now he understood the meaning of the name of his favorite bar. So much for the belief that we all share a common core of history and learning.

This morning I looked up the Hemlock Bar. It's in San Francisco. Very popular. I probably passed it last September when I was upping and downing on those treacherous hills linking the high-rise tech companies. He was probably sitting up there in a tiny cubby, bored out of his mind, answering dumb questions from other late-in-life writers. I am sure he scooted out promptly at five, to drink at the Hemlock. Shades of Socrates.

"Hey, Ya Got a Minute?"

Give me a minute.
Got a minute?
When was the last minute
you just
leaned back
and breathed?

Fingers weren't texting
Lips weren't speaking into your iPhone
Bluetooth wasn't finding itself
on your audio screen
in your Honda.

Yes, when was that minute?
It wasn't yesterday.
Wasn't last week.

Last season?
A year ago?

When did we lose control?

I hear that minute
jumping up and down
in the background of my sanity.
"Here I am.
Over here.
Look behind you."

Ah yes,
I remember it well.

Nitty Gritty and Nuance

team work

WE ALL WEAR OUT some days, trying to make sense of our lives, trying to make the puzzle pieces fit just right. These brief essays and poems provide a compact digestion of our absurdities, and allow me to play for a few minutes, to create a tweet-to-self, or change an absurdity to an answer. Perhaps at the very least, we can have a meaningful laugh that clears the brain.

Feng Shui for My Body

While I thumbed through old magazines, looking for a way to relax, start anew, and find world peace, my eye caught the title of an article on page thirty-two, *Feng Shui Updates for 2015*. Of course. That's it! Just the thing to keep me current and 'in the know' about anything that will balance my chakras, bring me wealth and prosperity beyond the fickle daily Illinois Lotto, and, best of all, lift my sags.

All at the same time. Show me the way!

I read on.

The 2015 Chinese New Year—the year of the Wood Sheep—started on February 19, just about the time I would have gladly lassoed the nearest Wood Sheep to carry me out of another unbearable Chicago winter.

As the article states, "2015 Feng Shui updates are used mostly with classical Feng Shui Bagua." I am to define the 'bagua of my space'.

My mind wanders.

Is it possible this stuff might work on the bagua of my neck, the bagua of my arms, the bagua of my knees? Surely hope so.

I turn the page. I learn that this particular annual Feng Shui update will prove most helpful, and will benefit avid practitioners as an "additional layer of energy, to help define the movement of good and bad energies" throughout their yearly travel.

According to the article, Feng Shui cures can be applied to my home, to "negate the possible unwelcome effects" in my home and life. So why not in my body?

Perfect. Let's begin! And-a-one, and-a-two...

Step 1 - HOME - Start with a clean and orderly home.

My translation: Wash your face and hands. *You gave up on the rest of the stuff years ago, so just skip it.*

Step 2 – HOME - Start in the East Feng Shui Bagua area, and then move clockwise.

Translation: Stand in the entryway of your home, face east, lift your left elbow up and out, at a sharp right angle to your body, until it becomes uncomfortable, and your armpit cries out for relief. Expect searing pain in fewer than three seconds.

Step 3 – BODY - Check your upper arms first. Note: They are easy to locate. They attach to your shoulders, and when raised and waved to and fro, they waddle like ducks. My grandchildren love them. The best Feng Shui cures for this area—to strengthen your overall success and good luck energy—are ones that express Metal and Water elements.

Translation: Find an old copper bracelet, one that never worked on your arthritis, hidden way back in your third-down dresser drawer, along with a seldom-used Disney spray-fan water bottle. Hold the bracelet while standing on one foot, singing "It's a Small World", squirting your upper arms with the spray bottle.

As you practice these movements and become more proficient in your arm-flapping and copper-bracelet-holding and water-bottle-brandishing, it is suggested that you branch out to provide additional healing through constructing intricate fountains and hanging large mirrors in this area in your home. This will increase the energy flow and decrease your sag.

Translation: Extra benefit to your Feng Shui cure routine can be achieved if you do your own lifting and carrying of the fountains and heavy mirrors. Energy abounds!

Warning! Avoid the introduction of any kind of Fire element into the routine described above. Why? The 2015 Southeast Feng Shui Bagua area has "challenging energy." Your decorating should involve Metal, Water, and Wood elements, so Fire would be a rather big no-no. This section in the article warns to limit 'constant noise, redecoration, or renovation' in this southeast area during 2015.

Here is where the "Shui" hits the "Feng"! How the heck am I to avoid the construction upheaval intended to benefit my 'east arms area' by adding mirrors and fountains, when my 'southeast-hips area' is attached directly below it, and I am not to 'upheave' that area this year?

I see contortion in my future.

Translation: Move on to other body areas, since my hips are most likely a no-go this year. I grow weary of this article, but I pause a moment to check my score so far, before turning the page to another absurd piece.

Final Score:

Wood Sheep	2	
Arms	0	(they are benched, awaiting the arrival of those fountains and mirrors)
Hips	0	(better luck next year)

Perhaps It's All Those Beeps I Hear

About halfway through my morning computer tasks, I heard that little beep that alerts me an email or text has just arrived. "Okay, but what's wrong with this?" that lonesome corner of my brain asked.

"What's wrong with this?" Lonesome Brain queried.

What's wrong? What's wrong? I'll tell you what's wrong! It defies sense, both common and unique. It's simply not prudent, wouldn't be, couldn't be, prudent! Bells. Bells should ding—ring-a-ling—chime— and resonate for major events and on special occasions, such as the wedding of your child who is definitely too young to get married, but you have plastered that smile on your face to make him or her feel you give your approval.

Or the bell that the teacher rings to call in the kids running amuck in the muck on the March playground, to save them from each other and themselves.

It was definitely appropriate to ring them at the end of that war that should have ended all wars but didn't, of course, manage to accomplish the call of all our soldiers home, forever and ever, never to visit foreign soil again. If only that one final bell chime at the end of Shostakovich's Symphony No. 15, Op. 141, would be the closing sound for our Congress each day that they managed again to procrastinate, without accomplishing a reasoned consensus, perhaps the world could right itself.

"My, aren't we in a tizzy, today! It was only a little ding, not a full ding-a-ling, no reverberation at all. See, there's nothing to worry about. Only a little ding!" Lonesome Brain tried to gloss over my angst as usual, but with little success.

"Not a full ding-a-ling? If it stopped me in my tracks, and opened YOU up, then it wears full ding-a-ling status, don't you think?" I replied.

Lonesome Brain had somewhat wearied over the years, with her multitasks of righting my ship, raising my mast right-angle-straight once more, fending off those reckless thought marauders, which were frequently dressed in colorful but obsessive garb. Occasionally I heard winsome sighs, as she held her breath to keep from shouting a brilliant psychological obscenity to me, to jerk me out of harm's way, barely a moment before my deck collapsed. Surely, she could handle today's soft ding—a ding which had somehow weighed a ton? Perhaps this was another last straw. There had been many of those over the years, and Lonesome Brain had quickly and carefully bent each one in two, and thrown them overboard without lifejackets, stuffing bouncy pink earplugs in her ears and mine, so we wouldn't hear their pleas.

Lonesome Brain tried her casual tactic mode.

"No, no I don't. It was only a slight sound. It should have been filed in our Background Noise Folder, you know, the one labeled 'Insensitive, Yet Harmless, Elevator Music?' Lonesome Brain frequently resorted to dumb humor trying to joke me out of the moment.

"Ha, not one of your best!" I responded. "The problem is that it really is a wakeup call. You see I had my two main tech items right next to me, my iPhone and my Mac. And then I heard that tiny alert ding from a distance. Where could it possibly be coming from? I remembered I had set the iPad out in the hall, so I would remember it for tomorrow's meeting.

At which precise moment did I transition from one, to two, and now to three tech products, with plugs, cords, earplugs, home and car chargers, and other assorted paraphernalia? Even an ordinary day for this nine-times-a-Granny entails almost the same amount of preparation and packing and carrying, as my own three toddlers necessitated 50 years ago…I almost need that large buggy to transport it all.

And here is my question for you, Lonesome Brain, "These tech traps…am I using them, or are they using me?"

Lonesome Brain fainted upon hearing my question. Perhaps when she awakes, she will answer me. Once it took three weeks. That is a very long time in any relationship. I'm not sure why she keeps me around.

Brand It, They Will Come
The New Age Writer
Humility Out, Bravado In

In the past
John Wayne did it.
On a ranch
In a movie
Somewhere in the West
Faded in memory...
Syncopated in a melody
Accompanied by clomping hooves.
While lone coyote howl notes
Bayed at wide open skies,
Cattle were claimed.

Today, a far greater chore
Notched on my writer's multitask belt.
I must brand it so they will come.

Not outriders after my cattle,
But hordes of ADMIRERS,
Seeking my words...
"BRAND your cattle,
In humble possession"

Translates now to
"Take that hot iron
Sizzle it well!
Lift it high,
Make it gel
Cast that spell."

Place logo just so.
No! Not on the rump
Nor on the shoulder,
Nor either side.
Just T-shirts and bookmarks,
And mugs and blogs,
Then pencils and postcards
Trinkets, and more.

You've Facebooked
You've Linked
You've Twittered
You've Blogged down!
Till nothing is left
To taint with your B-R-A-N-D.

Then one day it clicks,
You've conquered the query,
All your errors you fix,
Though you be so weary!

That awesome response
Emailed to Inbox with care,
"Dear Author, you're done,
You are *New Yorker* rare!"

Conway vs. Anime,
Passing It Forward

On January 8, 2014, our critique group was just leaving the Deerfield Barnes and Noble second floor location when a display table caught my eye. My humor idol's face graced the cover of his recently published book, *What's So Funny? My Hilarious Life*, by Tim Conway.

I stopped, and as always when a book speaks to me, I must reach out and touch it. I touched the cover, turned to fellow writer Barry, and shared my story of a lifelong 'fan-ship' admiration of Tim. Barry and I spoke briefly about the years of humor that Conway provided, and as we headed toward the escalator, I noticed a young man perusing the stacks near us. It occurred to me that even though the man was well past his teen years, he probably had no idea who Tim Conway was. Of course, to prove my point to myself, I asked him if he knew Tim. He smiled and responded, "No". I took a minute to explain Tim's place in America's comedy heritage, then I put on my sad face as Barry and I rode the escalator to the first floor.

Ten days later, my sixteen-year-old granddaughter, Samantha, and I were relaxing prior to calling it a day, after a homework session. We were waiting for the second episode of Season 4 of *Downton Abbey* to come on, and had time to kill. I headed for my computer. Sami headed to her phone. She wanted to expose me to her favorite current episode of an Anime, a fan-ship she had been following for some time.

Anime and I did not grow up together. I am even pre-Gilligan's Island and Sesame Street. I was stay-up-all-night-watching-snowy-fuzz-wrestling on our small television screen. The picture quality in my Iowa town with no television station, earned a 'D' most days in the late 1950s.

At first, I resisted Sami's encouragement, but then I recognized the perfect bargaining chip. That's it. Tim Conway. I told Sami I would watch the Anime episode if she would watch a Tim Conway YouTube moment in his "Old Man" routine on the *Carol Burnett Show*. We both were as enthusiastic about each other's genre as we would be with the prospect of cold porridge on a Chicago January morning. We holstered our angst, plastered some brave faux smiles on our faces, and hoped for the best, and if not the best, then at least the quickest!

I didn't even know if I would find Conway ammunition in my arsenal. But surely YouTube wouldn't fail me? You can always find the good, the bad, and the ugly there. Instantly, the myriad *Carol Burnett Show* "Old Man" skits appeared and we had choices, choices, choices—one after another. Less than four seconds into each skit, Sami had just the right reaction—loud, sustained laughter, no pause to breathe before clicking the next clip…then the next. Finally, she understood my earlier feeble prologue attempts to explain how all I had to see was the Old Man slow-walk shuffle and I would be consumed with laughter 'in the old days'. Who thought that one day Carol and Tim would be the old days?

And what is the rest of my story? Anime and I rode off into the sunset as BFF—Best Friends Forever? Well, not exactly.

When I took the time to look up information on Anime, my web search discovered that "what makes Anime immensely popular all over the world is its animations technique as well as the powerful storyline behind. Each character in these animations is strong and with a powerful personality. The storyline is gripping and one gets easily hooked on to those brilliant animations." (alikeminds.org)

Sami and her generation find the Anime characters and running plotlines as gripping as any stories that captured the generations before them. They love the artwork. They share the virtual challenges of the characters as if they are happening just up the street in their own neighborhoods. Sami mourns the killing off of a favored character just as we despise Julian Fellowes' dispensing of Matthew in the *Downton Abbey* series.

Sami and I meet in our passion and defense of our interests and the examples they provide for 'ships' (what Sami's generation calls relationships). I am so glad there is hope she and her peers may be coming out of Zombie-land adventures! Tim turned eighty years old last week.

Long live laughter and story, from generation to generation.

Thanks, Tim. Thanks, Sami.

What If?

What if
For just one day
We all forgot our labels

No Men, no Women
No Boys, no Girls
No Young, No Old
No Weak, No Bold

No Rich, No Poor, No Smart, No Slow
No White, No Black
No Republican
No Democrat

What if
For just one day
We stripped our paradigms from our minds
And took a closer look, between the lines
Where common sense and compassion reside

Dirty Pumpkin Chai

You have to be kidding! This is the name of something I am to ingest and digest at the big-name coffee house?

In the 1950s, if Mom had heard the term dirty pumpkin chai, she would have told me to "Scrub that pumpkin—stick it under running water and hose it off before bringing it in the house!"

And now, it's an upscale beverage term for grabbing all those sweet-type spices and mixing them with pumpkin flavoring. Do we even know what's in that syrup that probably has nothing to do with pumpkin? Then, after they drizzle this concoction with honey and charge mega-dollars, we sip slowly with graphic gusto, feeling upscale as the drink.

And what about that term 'chai'? Am I to pronounce it like a choo-choo sound or with a shush-shush sound? I've heard it both ways. Is there a tea-goddess who can zap me proficient in just the right 'tall-grandé-venti' size? Is there a coffee-shop-politically-correct-lingo dictionary? I want to appear to be in the know when I reach the front of the line and I say the NINE words to order what I want, prior to saying 'latté'.

And how will I ever say my request fast enough before the seven people standing behind me start to gripe and grumble at this seventy-five-year-old lady fumbling in her purse for the correct cash, with a few cents more for a tip.

"Dirty Pumpkin Chai, my eye!"

"You Buttered Your Bread, Now Sleep in It"

A Jiminy Cricket line from a 1940 *Pinocchio* film

Gone missing is that dapper and perky little cartoon guy with the umbrella that sat on Pinocchio's shoulder, providing wise counsel—counsel not always taken in time to prevent disaster. That advice said, "Don't do it. Wouldn't be prudent. Take another look. Avoid social media like the plague." Oops, all except that last one!

How do my coming-of-age grandkids decide to participate in these primary voting booth choices when our political role models out there have made such outrageous choices for their personal and professional lives? Indeed, the professional and personal are inextricably conjoined in one's behaviors. Why didn't they think before sending such inappropriate graphic private-part selfies? Certainly, the unwise and lavish decorating of one Peoria, Illinois, Congressman's private-public offices (to mimic a fictional British Yorkshire country estate of the post-Edwardian Era television show, *Downton Abbey*) might have been prevented by that tiny cartoon figure's advice, while perched on the loose-knee, strings-still-attached political puppet's shoulder.

At the very least, wouldn't you think a good friend or a good advisor might have played a part? And so, the nose grows.

Which box to choose?   How does a young voter come to trust leaders who can't judge the difference between private and public, in a time when there is no clearly marked barbed-wire divide between the two? What's in is out, and all the way out. April Fools…on a voting Primary day.

From Patio to Pity-o
An Iowa Girl's Lament Over a Slim Harvest
of Cherry Tomatoes Grown on Her Small Illinois Balcony

You can take the girl from the farm
Can you take the farm from the girl?
Spring bursts with hope
Buds all around
Home Depot sale beckons
Removes her frown.

Paltry pickings as June closes
Why choose vegetables over roses?
Ten inches high in such a lovely pot
Nurture or nature,
Green thumb she's got,
Squeezes it into last year's glove.

Water hand-carried out the balcony door
Just enough to avoid neighbors below
A summer of perfect sun
Ten hours each day
Careful to rotate
Watches her crop climb.

Bounty begins, slowly at first
Patience she spends – anticipates reward
Red skies at night
Salad's delight
How many you ask?
She savors each one... of seventy-eight.

Cubs Win – November 2, 2016

Throughout this playoff season, I was drawn to relief pitcher Aroldis Chapman's serious and determined face, each time he was brought in to pick up the pieces. What a delight to see him display that gigantic smile as the Cubs finally pulled it off.

Nothing shows patience and hope
Like the faces of Cub fans
Throughout the years.

What a game that was
The only thing missing
Was a good old Chicago snowstorm
To turn Wrigley Field white
To match those long-loyal fans' hair.

But then we've had
108 years of those
So, this time we opted
For only
A mild rain delay.

"Hey, Chicago, whaddaya say?"
"The Cubs WON today!"

What makes me think I am a valid seventy-eight-year-old sports reporter?

My extensive hands-on baseball contact.

Age eleven—backyard game, playing catcher, way up too close to the batter, in my friends' yard.

Oops—great swing, all eyes on the ball—except mine. My eye was on the bat. Yes, ON the bat. Nine stitches on the frontal bone of my left eyebrow. Wanna see my scar? I followed the game much more closely after that, but saw my future positions better played in the outfield, where there was time to prepare, or at least duck, before a ball was hit. Describes my philosophy for life.

Then there was the time my daughter, Michelle, was teaching her son, Max, to pitch, and he threw her a perfect strike—directly at her nose. My bad—I must have forgotten to warn her to play outfield ... *TRADITION!*

Say Nay to the Fray

Stay above the fray, you say?
Can't, it draws me in
Each way, each day.

Arrows sharply aim my way.
Possible escape?
No way, this day.

Stay above the fray, you say?
Arm's distance,
Okay?

Nay, too close,
Twill surely singe.
Then twist and dodge,
Watch them unhinge.

Stay above the fray, I pledge!
Senses trained
Form careful wedge.

Game of wits, led by truth
Pawns stand fast
Shields in place
Arms entwined, tight embrace.

Stay above the fray, you said?
I will,
As soon as *they*
Have fled!

Breaking News

This label may have been sitting on my television screen for an hour or two, or a day or two. Maybe even longer. It is posted for as long as it seems feasible, to wring every drop of lure and lurid from its beckoning. It pulls even us savvy sailors into it, unwitting and drugged with the promise of "Extra, extra, see all about it!"

It should more aptly be termed 'Breaking Olds', based on the length of its use. Perhaps it makes sense to post it so continuously, to accommodate our constant channel-changing fingertips, flipping from site to site in fear of missing the important stuff, desiring to be the first to know.

Its use mimics my overuse of exclamation points in my writing—when you use them so frequently, they lose their impact. Seen one, seen 'em all.

In the old days, we could relegate the news to chosen times, to integrate calm Sunday morning paper reading into our busy schedules, turning pages and selecting articles that spoke to us in more quiet tones. Less blatant. Unobtrusive. Face-to-face conversation was maintained with those around us, even if only a "Honey, did you see this?"

Today's news shouts and jumps up and down like sugar-high toddlers demanding our immediate attention, feeding our millennial need for excitement and entertainment with each click.

I wonder who decides when the 'Breaking News' topic has fulfilled its mission, and needs to be displaced by the 'Breaking Newer'? I want that job. I'd exercise a much stronger whip, to remove each topic quickly, within an hour or so, avoiding the mold and mildew that grows with each passing minute, clogging our brains.

The New Downton Abbey Season
SPOILER ALERT!

1. SEASON 6 WILL BE THE FINAL SEASON
2. The characters will all have an English accent
3. There will be twists and turns in every relationship
4. A few kisses will sizzle
5. The staircase will go up and down
6. The servants will talk together in the servant quarters … or nickel and dime it, in the hushed hallways
7. The grounds will be green and lush
8. There will be a lush drunk in at least one episode
9. The people you want to get together will keep missing each other
10. Etc., etc., etc.
11. *Sounds like Shakespeare, doesn't it!*

My Desktop – Ad Infinitum

Surfaces, surfaces, surfaces
I love them.
They complete me.
If a new one appears in my abode
I rush to eliminate its smooth polish
Or worn wood
Or granite
Or plastic laminate.

In a flash, I gravitate
To cover every last quarter-inch
With notes, mail, baubles and bangles.
Yesterday's grocery list
Aided and abetted by last month's
Undone
TO-DO LIST.

No wonder at the end of another tax year
As I scurry and worry

To find that final lost piece of
Whatever will prove to be
Most assuredly,
A NON-deductible,
I scoop it all up and swear under my breath
While resolving, one more time,
"NEXT YEAR, I WILL BE ORGANIZED."

Just One Word

At your story's end,
If they speared just one word
To describe you,
Would you want that word to be 'thorough'?
Maybe—but I think not.
So, no, most definitely not.

Thorough won't arouse
Legions of lovers,
Doesn't cause tingly feelings along a softly shaved neckline.
It simply says completed, finished, done.
No hearts there to be won.

Thorough says schoolmarm 100 percent,
T's crossed, I's dotted.
Marked the grade in the tiny box.
"Left face, right face, close your hall locker locks."

Of course not, not that word.
Choose the best one she ever heard.

PEARLS *and* KNOTS

One to charm and frame forever
A huge and wondrous open smile.

Expansive passion airy and light,
Not afraid to capture the night.
A term to raise eyebrows
To just their right height.

That's it, on the tip of your tongue,
A word for all life's soldiers,
This search is
Done.

LAUGHTER,
That's it!
That's her number one.

Sweet Snippets

Faith, Courage, Chocolate—I had these three words carved on Otto's stone, to describe his character and to make us all smile through our sadness when we visited his gravesite. Otto went through so many challenges steadied by those first two traits, ever present in his personality. He always made sure his chocolate (European dark only, of course) could be found, even though I always hid it high in a cupboard, so he wouldn't over-do, as he tasted life's sweetness.

My daughter Michelle's husband, Steve, shared something hilarious with my other daughter, Leigha, and me, as the four of us visited Otto's newly placed gravestone for the first time. After taking several deep breaths to gather our thoughts and our courage, we held hands and went around our circle, telling a memory. When Steve's turn came, he looked skyward for a few quiet seconds, and in a perfect mimic of Otto's accent, implored...

"VHY, Otto? VHY did you have to leave me here—all alone, vithout you—vith these three strong VOMEN?" Steve broke our tension perfectly. Otto would have loved that moment and Steve's dramatic delivery.

FOOT-note: How do you make a podiatrist? Mix one large yard, one electric lawnmower being pushed by one teenage boy at high speed. Then back up too quickly, to make the perfect green grass swath, while forgetting that last year you built the perfect raised vegetable garden. It was only a small piece of my son Michael's big toe, but the expert care of the podiatric doctor inspired a teenager's career choice a few years later. Mike has saved many toes and legs, since.

One Last Word

Wishing I could Abracadabra a do-over. The first thing I would magically zap with my wishing wand would occur at the age of seven. I would decide at that precipitous age to prepare to write my late-life memoir. I'd start a journal that never happened in real life. I'd write letters to myself of important-or-not-so daily events, and hide them in a binder that was NOT entitled "Diary"—too tempting to open if found under my bed, or wedged way back in my dark closet.

I'd be careful and secretive. I'd not tell a soul that I would one day write a memoir whether I became famous or not. But I would definitely have the common sense to know that some of my memories were important or fun enough to record for posterity.

I am sure I was much too busy planning to raid the chocolate chip cookie table on the way to my birth, so I must have missed taking advantage of the "common sense-DNA" table. So, in this next go-round, I plan to grab just enough hints to plan ahead, to give my seven-year-old self the foresight to prepare for the lifelong mission of saving, savoring and sharing life's lessons, with just enough humor and more than enough details—details not clouded in fuzzy forgotten phrases—in order to astound and encourage others to write their own truths, perhaps sprinkled with a few harmless fictions for spice.

Dream on, Sarah.

ACKNOWLEDGMENTS

KEEPING PACE WITH THE SPEED of traffic in our lives requires paying close attention to our moments of light, learning how to make them flicker long enough to clearly illumine our pathways. What fun it is to stroll on a summer eve, watching fireflies spark the night briefly and then move on.

Often those bright moments morph into lean leopards that challenge our decisions and force us onto another route. Scary or threatening at first, they provide strong reasons to shift our thinking and we grow. In spite of our desire to remain fixed in place, we adapt, then become comfortable in our new knowledge.

Writing a memoir—even a quirky one like this—feels like such a public baring of a few moments in my life. I have always dueled with my shy nature, winning some battles and losing others. Having served in many public capacities in my professional life, I have been careful to protect the privacy of students and teachers and staff. I am deeply indebted to the students and parents I have served. I have learned so much from them. This memoir is not a tell-all; it is a tell *some*, in hopes of encouraging others to remember their own moments, and write them down.

Many thanks to all my family members and firefly friends and leopards, for your love, guidance and humor, from Dubuque, to Peoria, Chicago,

Overland Park, Kansas, Milwaukee, Glenview, Buffalo Grove, Gurnee, Mundelein and Libertyville. From my earliest Dubuque days at Lincoln, Bryant, Washington Schools, and on to Dubuque Senior High School, so many friends and classmates anchored my first eighteen years. Our Class of 1957 blessed my years in Dubuque, and our reunions, anchored by William Howes and his crew of tireless home-towners (thanks to Judy Edmonds and Beverly Graves and all others) since our graduation, taught me to cherish the times we shared.

I extend my deepest gratitude to my children: Leigha Kinnear, Michael Schwarcz, and Michelle Schwarcz-Haubrich. They have provided magical moments of astonishment and laughter throughout their young and mature years. They always make me proud and honored to love them and learn from them, just like when they asked, well past their bedtime, "One more time around the coffee table, please, Mom?"

Special thanks to grandchildren Rebecca, Samantha, Max, and Maya. All fine writers from an early age, they live close by and have served as my car-captive beta readers, critiquing some pieces, while we drove back and forth to swimming, drama, and choir competitions. In the background, I always hear mega-reader Maya's sound advice, especially her age 14 admonition to "avoid the information-dump, G-Ma!" There are not enough words to thank Samantha, who painted the cover for this memoir, weaving my memories into a delightful visual story of its own, joining fantasy with reality. And to Rebecca, whose life-saving talents unfortunately had to extend to her own 'save', in her disastrous accident on Lake Michigan. She follows in her Grandpa's strong survival footsteps.

My career as a Teacher and Principal in the Chicago Public Schools (Volta, Sauganash, and Solomon Schools); West Oak Middle School, in Mundelein, Illinois; Ida Crown Jewish Academy in Chicago, Illinois; and Ramona Elementary School in Wilmette, Illinois, allowed me to work with outstanding staff who were always passionate and professional in supporting children's lives and learning. Catherine Z. Smith stands as the role model for outstanding teacher, principal, team player and friend. Kathleen and Robert Sandlass, Gene Mitofsky, Phyllis Markovich, Julienne Williams, Raynell Walls, Rita Burton, Patricia Cegielski, Patricia Green, Rabbi Dr. Leonard Matanky, Rabbi Michael Myers, Daniel Harris, Cynthia Levin, Shelley Stopek, Sarah Wainkrantz, Sheri Goldstein, Tirza Kahan, Susan Sennett, Shellie Strimling, Marlene Wasserstrom, Breanna Piland, Nancy Berg, Gail Heckmyer, Hope Sohn, Minda G. Smith, Sandra Baenziger, Sandy Karwowski, and Debbie Greer represent just a few staff of a very long and revered list of dedicated professionals with whom I served for forty-two years, as we carried out our mission to reach each child every day. Thank you all! You are outstanding.

I am grateful to the members, workshop authors, editors, and publishers of the Off Campus Writers Workshop, in Winnetka, Illinois. OCWW is the oldest continuously running writing group in America. Their weekly workshops have filled me with instruction and encouragement in the craft and art of the writing process.

I am indebted to my writing-editing buddies, Kelley Chikos (author of *Trickle-Down Teaching: A Lighthearted Romp Through the Minefield of Your Rookie Year*) and Maureen O'Grady. They have provided invaluable insight these past several years, along with such gentle instruction in the intricacies of creativity. Best of all has been their supportive advice to persevere and take a risk. Maureen's meticulous research of what people treasure in their lives needs to be a book of its own one day.

Estelle Laughlin (author of *Transcending Darkness: A Girl's Journey Out of the Holocaust*; and *Hannah, I Forgot to Tell You*) has provided amazing encouragement and inspiration, teaching me to appreciate the challenges and the blessings of writing in equal measure.

All my writing critique group members—Barry Chessick, Lyle Cohen, Richard Davidson, Kathy DeNicolo, Judith Godfrey, Buzzie Lieberman,

Judy Panko-Reis, Peter Slonek—deserve high-fives-times-ten, for their outstanding advice, humor, and friendship as we share our questions and brainstorm creative writing guidance in lively discussions twice each month, over these past seven years. Led by researcher extraordinaire, Brenda Rossini, their extensive knowledge and various careers in multiple fields, along with writing and literature, provide a master seminar for us on Wednesdays, with Judy and Sheldon's dining room hospitality.

I appreciate the expert guidance of publishing consultant Kim Bookless in her exciting self-publishing workshops in the Chicago area. Through Kim, I found Gwyn of GKS Creative, who has taken this memoir from nearly done, to finished and published. Thank you! Thank you!

And to Otto's doctors: I cannot thank you enough for your outstanding care for Otto for eighteen years—particularly, Dr. Howard Katz and Dr. Michael Lewis. You are proof that medicine is an art as well as a science. I am in awe of your patience and wisdom. And to Mary Mwange for her superb care for Otto through his most challenging years in Gurnee; your heart and skills are always in the right place.

163

Maximilian Schwarcz

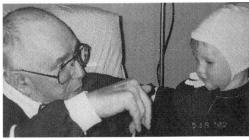

173

ABOUT THE AUTHOR

AFTER A LONG CAREER AS A Teacher and Principal in the Chicago Public Schools, and Teacher and Public Relations Coordinator in Diamond Lake Schools in Mundelein, Illinois, Sarah Schwarcz traded in her chalk to write and share a few of her life stories in her memoir, *Pearls and Knots*. One of Sarah's highest honors is a student's comment on how to survive her class: "Stay focused, and above all—laugh at her jokes!"

For many years Sarah directed her side-gig writing interests to education projects. With her daughter, Leigha Kinnear, she co-authored a national PTA trainer workshop to increase parent involvement. Sarah designed and directed *Kids Convention*, one of the earliest computer-interactive children's programs of fifty-two Chicagoland schools, for the Kohl Children's Museum in Glenview, Illinois.

She previously served as Publicity/Communications Coordinator for the weekly Off Campus Writers Workshop (oldest continuously running writing workshop in the U.S.) sessions in Winnetka, Illinois, where she continues to have valuable access to outstanding authors, agents and publishing information.

Picking 'just one' of anything has always been a challenge for Sarah, so her writing endeavors include memoir, middle-grade fantasy (watch for her new one this coming year) and poetry. She intends to chocolate-brownie-bribe all her grandchildren—Baila, Adam, Aryeh, Zachary, Tuvia, Rebecca, Samantha, Maximilian, and Maya— and her great-grands—Rivka, Zevy, Shaya, and Talia—to read her books, if they don't pick them up on their own.

Some summers Sarah helps her daughter, Michelle, keep adorable, wriggly newborn Rhodesian Ridgebacks in clean laundry and cuddles. Winston, Sarah's ten-pound Miniature Wire-Haired Dachshund, commands the home fort when Sarah wanders out. (Shush! Please don't tell Winston he's not a Great Dane!)

Visit Sarah's website and blog at **pearlsandknots.com**.